MW01517891

Truth Tried and Triumphant
By: Gordon Rumford

Copyright ©2015
978-1-927684-20-7
Published by
Freedom Press International Inc.
12-111 Fourth Ave., Ste 185 St. Catharines, ON L2S 3P5

Cover Design by Cam Rumford
www.northernfoxdesigns.com

Jesus Wept

Jesus wept,
Jesus died.
Humiliated - Crucified.

Willingly,
Bearing Blame.
My transgression - His deep shame.

Gladly offered,
Lifted high.
Lord of heaven - heard his cry.

Jesus risen,
Life restored.
Throned in glory - death no more.

Blood outpouring,
Hope conceived.
Ardent prayer - grace received.

Broken hearted,
Bended knee.
Fully reconciled to Thee.

—*Susan Rumford, ©1995*

DEDICATION

For Susan
My ever present encouraging companion
who knows me and still
believes in me.

Proverbs 31:29 NIV
"Many women do noble things,
but you surpass them all."

TABLE OF CONTENTS

ENDORSEMENTS

In John's vision of heavenly worship in Revelation 5, we hear the heavenly throng declaring that the death of Jesus was in fact a powerful act that redeemed an uncountably great multitude. Gordon Rumford's book describing that passion of our Lord helps us to see that what looked like an experience of a helpless man was actually the deliberate obedience of the only man who could control his own destiny. Providing the cultural details that underlie the narrative, the book causes the story of Jesus' passion to come alive in many ways. This is a fresh narration of the suffering of the one who loved us and gave himself for us, and the author deserves our thanks for his fresh retelling of the story that never grows old. - *Dr. Stan Fowler*

In Truth Tried and Triumphant, Gordon Rumford combines his interest in history and his love for the Lord in an exploration of the last hours of Jesus' ministry on behalf of humanity. His facility with language and attention to detail bring freshness to a subject with which most Christians are already quite familiar. He has drawn together interesting historical facts and cultural details to help the reader understand nuances in the gospel record that might otherwise be overlooked. Readers in the early centuries of the Christian movement would have immediately caught these subtleties from the text, but time and trends have clouded them for us.

The book's accessible style allows the reader to proceed quickly from chapter to chapter, yet its depth and breadth encourage them to go slowly and savour the insights. The probing questions at the end of each chapter provide an opportunity for personal reflection and application—prompting the reader to consider both cultural assumptions and personal complacency. If read as intended, Truth Tried and Triumphant will not only inform your mind and deepen your devotion, but will actually promote your being more like its subject.

Read this book if you enjoy having your mind stretched and your heart touched. - *Ron Hughes*

ACKNOWLEDGMENTS

Several people should receive special mention as I reflect on those who cheered me on with this book that took parts from 10 years to write. Stephen Berghofer B. Sc., M.D., CIC., longtime friend, frequently reignited my sometime lagging spirits surrounding this project. Without his gentle, cheerful and timely interventions the project might have been lost. His daughter-in-law, Katherine Berghofer B.A., M.A., used her English major to good effect in helping edit the manuscript. I am thankful for her participation, even though it was from a distance and I have yet to meet her face to face. Dianne Tyers M.A., M.B.A., another family friend, did much to assist me in my research to add historical and cultural content. She also did much to help me sharpen the Reflections.

Of course I take full responsibility personally for any errors of grammar and factual content.

ABOUT THE AUTHOR

Gordon Rumford, H.B.A., M.A., L.'Ih., began ministering in the Christian community in 1966 upon graduation from Seminary. His love of the Scriptures and its history and culture has led him to include such content in his preaching and teaching which has taken him to churches and conferences in Canada, the U.S.A., Ecuador, the U.K., and Malawi. He strives to instill in his listeners to sense that "they are right there" in the biblical narrative. This book is the product of many years of informal and formal study and research. Gordon continues to minister weekends in various churches. He mentors younger pastors as they face the many challenges of ministry. Also he has developed a special interest in the pastoral care of people in pain of various kinds. His recreational passions include astro-photography, reading in astronomy, physics, and history, all the while enjoying the company of his numerous grandchildren.

BOOK SUMMARY

In a Greek exegesis class in 1965 Gordon Rumford discovered that in John 18:8 Jesus actually commanded the arresting officers to let His followers go! In other words, Jesus told the police what they could and could not do. In being taken captive, the Lord Jesus takes captive His captors. Taking this truth as a template, Gordon laid it over the various subsequent scenes to see how they too demonstrated that our Lord controlled and triumphed in every situation right up to the moment He dismissed His spirit in death on the cross. Using this lens to sharpen the bible-reader's focus on the Savior, Gordon explores how much there is to marvel at, and how much cause for worship and praise to come from the reader's lips. You are invited to join Gordon on his journey in the Gospels from the Upper Room to Golgotha and to fall in love with your Lord and your God all over again.

INTRODUCTION

John 3:16
For God so loved the world that he gave his
one and only Son, that whoever believes in him
shall not perish but have eternal life.

Ephesians 1:4-5
For he chose us in him before the creation of the world to be holy
and blameless in his sight. In love he predestined us for adoption
to sonship through Jesus Christ, in accordance with his pleasure
and will—

The entire Bible, from Genesis to Revelation, is the story of God's love for
all of creation, including His love for us, and His quest to bring us back to
Him. Upon casting out Adam and Eve from the Garden of Eden, because
they'd sinned by eating forbidden fruit, God promised to send a Savior
who would destroy Satan and rescue humanity from evil. Throughout
the Old Testament, increasing numbers of assurances were spoken by
prophets of God's chosen people, the Jews. Jesus did come at last to fulfill
all these prophecies. In doing so, He paid the ultimate price for our sins,
and demonstrated God's great love for us.

This book draws from the four Gospel witnesses of Jesus' last hours with
His disciples, as well as the agony He endured on our behalf at the hands
of both Jews and Gentiles. It's a common misconception that Jesus was
an inert prisoner, a mere victim of His capture and ultimate crucifixion.
While exploring this book, you'll discover that Jesus was, in fact, master of
both His life and death. Although physically captive, the Savior dominated
His enemies and He proved to be the One in charge of every situation
right through His crucifixion. Through His silence, subtlety of expression,
exposure of hypocrisy, knowledge of Scripture, and astonishing grace,
Jesus' captors were utterly confounded as the crucifixion progressed. His
conduct, despite brutal injustice, provides present day Christians with a
powerful model of behavior—a standard to strive for while navigating this
often unjust world. Each chapter of this book covers a distinct event in
Jesus' persecution, beginning with the Last Supper and concluding with

Jesus' spirit rising from the cross. This study will specifically examine Jesus' capture, trials, and ultimate execution. The biblical text from the New International Version (NIV) is the foundation for the Gospel writers' narrative insights. Like witnesses in a courtroom testifying to a common event, each Gospel writer shares his unique perspective gospels of the divine story. Thus, this book will draw you back and forth among the four to help you understand the overall story in a new and more comprehensive light.

Throughout the reading, you'll encounter interesting historical and cultural facts meant to enliven the material and afford a tangible sense of being present in Jesus' life and death. At the same time, some interpretive and dramatic license has been taken to engage the mind and spirit as fully as possible. At the conclusion of each chapter, a personal reflection is provided. Its purpose is to challenge, and evaluate your perception of the events and re-evaluate your own moral character and conduct in light of Jesus' example.

It's impossible to adequately describe Jesus' suffering, since nothing we've ever witnessed or endured can compare to it. No one has suffered so much, nor loved so unconditionally. Even so, examining the circumstances of Jesus' trials helps us to recognize His remarkable nature and the magnitude of the personal sacrifice He made for us. As you read and digest this information, I hope you'll gain a greater understanding of the love your Creator and His Son have for you.

Come with us now to the road of the cross, and listen to Jesus and the disciples as they walk together.

Chapter 1

THE LAST SUPPER

Matthew 26:17-19
On the first day of the Festival of Unleavened Bread, the disciples
came to Jesus and asked, "Where do you want us to make
preparations for you to eat the Passover?" He replied, "Go into the
city to a certain man and tell him, 'The Teacher says: My appointed
time is near. I am going to celebrate the Passover with my disciples
at your house.' " So the disciples did as Jesus had directed them and
prepared the Passover.

Excitement filled the air as the Jews prepared for the Passover. Each year,
they looked forward to the pilgrimage to Jerusalem and the festivities that
would occur throughout the week. Tens of thousands of pilgrims would
crowd the city. Many would have to pitch their tents and camp outside the
city walls on the surrounding hills as Jerusalem became overcrowded.

Passover commemorates the Israelites liberation from Egypt, as told in
Exodus 12. God had instructed the Israelites to use the blood of a lamb
to mark the doors of their homes so that the Angel of Death would "pass
over" them. As punishment on the Egyptians, who would not free the
Israelites, God moved through Egypt killing their firstborn sons. Yet He
passed over the Israelite homes that were marked with lamb's blood. After
this night of bereavement, the Egyptian Pharaoh allowed the Israelites to
leave Egypt.

The seven-day celebration of Passover begins with a great feast on the first
evening. The Jews gather with their families for the Passover meal, also
known as the "*seder*." The *seder*, which is Hebrew for "order," recalls the
last meal in Egypt before the Hebrews embarked on their journey to the
Promised Land. The meal includes lamb, wine, bitter herbs, and unleavened
bread. The traditional foods commemorate the ancient customs, while the

bitter herbs represent the bitterness of their captivity.

Passover is then followed by a week-long celebration called the Feast of Unleavened Bread. During the Exodus from Egypt, the Israelites had to flee so rapidly that they were unable to wait for their bread to rise properly. Instead, they baked their bread without yeast.

John 13:4-20

So [Jesus] got up from the meal, took off his outer clothing, and wrapped a towel around his waist. After that, he poured water into a basin and began to wash his disciples' feet, drying them with the towel that was wrapped around him.

He came to Simon Peter, who said to him, "Lord, are you going to wash my feet?" Jesus replied, "You do not realize now what I am doing, but later you will understand." "No," said Peter, "you shall never wash my feet." Jesus answered, "Unless I wash you, you have no part with me." "Then, Lord," Simon Peter replied, "not just my feet but my hands and my head as well!"

Jesus answered, "Those who have had a bath need only to wash their feet; their whole body is clean. And you are clean, though not every one of you." For he knew who was going to betray him, and that was why he said not every one was clean.

When he had finished washing their feet, he put on his clothes and returned to his place. "Do you understand what I have done for you?" he asked them. "You call me 'Teacher' and 'Lord,' and rightly so, for that is what I am. Now that I, your Lord and Teacher, have washed your feet, you also should wash one another's feet. I have set you an example that you should do as I have done for you. Very truly I tell you, no servant is greater than his master, nor is a messenger greater than the one who sent him. Now that you know these things, you will be blessed if you do them.

"I am not referring to all of you; I know those I have chosen. But this is to fulfill this passage of Scripture: 'He who shared my bread has turned against me.' "I am telling you now before it happens, so that when it does happen you will believe that I am who I am. Very truly I tell you, whoever accepts anyone I send accepts me; and whoever accepts me accepts the one who sent me."

Aside: During Jesus' time, it was customary for the host to anoint his guests' heads with oil, offer them water, kiss them, bless them, and bring them into his house. Then, the host's servants would wash the guests' feet. If the host wished to honor his guests, he would wash their feet himself.

Jesus gathered His disciples together for the Passover meal, for they were His family. As the festivities progressed, an argument broke out among them concerning which should be considered the greatest (Luke 22:24). With such an attitude, who would wash their feet? The twelve disciples did not have a servant to carry out this humble task, and apparently none of them was willing to perform the service for the others. In response to this argument, Jesus rose from the table, knelt beside each disciple and cleansed his feet.

When Jesus began to perform the servant's task, the disciples were embarrassed. An uneasy silence fell over the room until Jesus came to Peter. Peter was adamant that Jesus would not wash his feet. Jesus replied, "You do not realize now what I am doing but later you will understand." This was a wonderful statement to Peter, for Jesus meant to assure Peter to trust in His actions and although Peter did not realize their importance in that moment, later he would understand. However, Peter stubbornly refused, saying that his feet would never be washed by Jesus. Jesus quickly responded to Peter with a powerful ultimatum. Either he would submit to having his feet washed, or he wouldn't reside with Jesus. This stunned Peter, who then gave in to Jesus fully saying, "Bathe me entirely!" Jesus then washed the feet of all twelve disciples, including Judas who would soon walk the path of betrayal.

By completing this humble duty, Jesus demonstrated to the disciples that they must possess humility and perform even the lowliest tasks for one another. He challenged them to be willing servants for the sake of the people; to abstain from petty arguments and to share the Word of God.

Jesus said that He expected the disciples to behave with similar grace and He would bless them for following this teaching on humility and service.

John 13:21-30

After he had said this, Jesus was troubled in spirit and testified, "Very truly I tell you, one of you is going to betray me."

His disciples stared at one another, at a loss to know which of them he meant. One of them, the disciple whom Jesus loved, was reclining next to him. Simon Peter motioned to this disciple and said, "Ask him which one he means."

Leaning back against Jesus, he asked him, "Lord, who is it?"

Jesus answered, "It is the one to whom I will give this piece of bread when I have dipped it in the dish." Then, dipping the piece of bread, he gave it to Judas, the son of Simon Iscariot. As soon as Judas took the bread, Satan entered into him.

So Jesus told him, "What you are about to do, do quickly." But no one at the meal understood why Jesus said this to him. Since Judas had charge of the money, some thought Jesus was telling him to buy what was needed for the festival, or to give something to the poor. As soon as Judas had taken the bread, he went out. And it was night.

When Jesus told the disciples that one among them was a traitor, they weren't just embarrassed; they were also confused and agitated. Which disciple could Jesus possibly mean? Who would turn against Him and why? Who would betray His trust, friendship, and discipleship? As disciples, they'd learned to preach the Word of God. They'd been graced with the power to perform miracles. They'd been sent out in pairs to teach and minister. Who would turn their back on all this? Each of them, with the exception of Judas, wondered if he could unknowingly be the guilty one.

Jesus had blessed Judas' ministry and shown him the same compassion as the other disciples during their three and a half years together. Judas was accorded the additional honor of being made treasurer of the twelve followers. At the Passover meal, Jesus offered Judas the seat of honor beside Him and gave him the sop, the best piece of food at the meal. Traditionally, the sop was reserved for the person the host most wanted to distinguish. The other disciples were never suspicious of Judas because of the favours Jesus bestowed on him. This made Judas' betrayal all the more unthinkable.

These events transpired on Thursday night, or Jewish Friday. On the previous Tuesday evening, Judas had gone to the chief priests, reaching an agreement to surrender Jesus for thirty pieces of silver (Matthew 26:14-16). This was the customary price paid for a slave (Zechariah 11:12). Judas arranged to expose Jesus at a time when very few of His followers would be present (Luke 22:6).

> Matthew 26:26-28
> While they were eating, Jesus took bread, and when he had given thanks, he broke it and gave it to his disciples, saying, "Take and eat; this is my body."
>
> Then he took a cup, and when he had given thanks, he gave it to them, saying, "Drink from it, all of you. This is my blood of the covenant, which is poured out for many for the forgiveness of sins.

Jesus often used metaphors when teaching His disciples. For example, He referred to Himself as a door (John 10:7), the light (John 9:5), and bread (John 6:41). Eating the bread and drinking the wine were to become the symbols of their participation in Jesus' sacrifice. Traditionally, the Israelites of the Old Testament laid hands on sacrificial animals before offering them to God or sending them off into the wilderness. Today, the metaphor of Jesus as the Bread of Life is remembered during communion as Christians eat the bread of His body and drink the wine of His blood. Just as bread and wine feed and nourish our bodies, so the body and blood of Jesus feed and nourish our souls.

In my view it was necessary for Jesus to dismiss Judas prior to breaking bread with the other disciples. Judas was not one of Jesus' true followers and therefore, would not be delivered by His death on the cross (John

17:12). Judas' presence at the breaking of the bread would have tainted its sanctity. Communion is a holy meal, reserved for Christians. They're delivered from sin by Jesus' sacrifice.

John 13: 33
My children, I will be with you only a little longer. You will look for me, and just as I told the Jews, so I tell you now: Where I am going, you cannot come.

To add to the disciples' distress, Jesus went on to explain that He was leaving them and they couldn't come with Him. This was terrible news for they relied on His physical presence. Leading to this moment, however, Jesus had been mentoring the disciples, arming them with the teachings needed to continue their own good works. Through His guidance, Jesus sought to establish the foundation for the ministry that would flourish after His death.

John 13: 37-38
Peter asked, "Lord, why can't I follow you now? I will lay down my life for you." Then Jesus answered, "Will you really lay down your life for me? Very truly I tell you, before the rooster crows, you will disown me three times!"

Finally, in front of all of the disciples, Jesus told Peter that he was going to deny Jesus not once, but three times before dawn. Peter would deny knowing Jesus. He would disown Him. The disciples could hardly believe their ears. This was Peter, the man who set a strong example and took initiative. In fact, his name meant "rock." What could possibly convince Peter to deny Jesus? Suddenly, the future seemed darker than before. The disciples wondered what dangers the coming hours would bring. To reassure them, Jesus began teaching them many incredible things. All of John 14-17 was teaching on how to calm their troubled hearts and after the resurrection would not only feed their faith but give them the needed courage to pursue their ministry even in the face of death.

John 14:2-3
My Father's house has many rooms; if that were not so, would I

have told you that I am going there to prepare a place for you? And if I go and prepare a place for you, I will come back and take you to be with me that you also may be where I am.

Jesus immediately told the disciples that His departure would be for their benefit. He would be preparing a place for them in Heaven in His absence. When the time came, He would return to gather the disciples, and they would live eternally in the Promised Land. He assured the men that their separation was only temporary—an everlasting life would be their future with God. To ease their great apprehension, Jesus explained that they would have a wonderful ministry in His absence and one that would exceed anything He had accomplished during the three and a half years that they had walked together with Him. They would be wonderfully productive and live blessed and meaningful lives! Then they left the Upper Room and began the walk to Gethsemane.

John 15: 1-2, 5, 10, 11

I am the true vine, and my Father is the gardener. He cuts off every branch in me that bears no fruit, while every branch that does bear fruit he prunes so that it will be even more fruitful.

I am the vine; you are the branches. If you remain in me and I in you, you will bear much fruit; apart from me you can do nothing.

If you keep my commands, you will remain in my love, just as I have kept my Father's commands and remain in his love. I have told you this so that my joy may be in you and that your joy may be complete.

In the Old Testament, Israel is referred to multiple times as a "fruitless vine." Jesus, emphasizing that He was the true vine, stressed that He would bear fruit. Jesus used the allegory of the vine and the branches to illustrate to the disciples that He and His followers had a vital and living union though He was physically absent from them. Beyond His crucifixion, their union in the Spirit would preserve the strength of the branches. In Scripture, pruning denotes a method of facilitating healthy growth. In this case, stunted growth is symbolic of disobedience; productive growth is the product of God pruning and our obedience. Faith and trust in Jesus would allow the disciples to celebrate His love and experience the joy of the Spirit in their walk. Despite these reassurances, the disciples felt utterly joyless learning of Jesus' looming betrayal, Peter's soon denial of Jesus and especially the Lord's departure.

John 16:2

They will put you out of the synagogue; in fact, the time is coming when anyone who kills you will think they are offering a service to God.

Jesus then warned the disciples about the coming persecution, which would occur at the hands of the Jews and make martyrs of those responsible for God's good works. In this moment, there is a bittersweet note to His teaching. While the disciples' ministry would nurture faith and the spiritual prosperity of the followers in Christ, their successes depended on the harsh reality of Jesus' persecution. In the years after Jesus' death, the persecutors would turn against His disciples, who, in turn, would sacrifice their own lives to exalt the Savior.

John 16:7-11, 13, 14

But very truly I tell you, it is for your good that I am going away. Unless I go away, the Advocate will not come to you; but if I go, I will send him to you. When he comes, he will prove the world to be in the wrong about sin and righteousness and judgment: about sin, because people do not believe in me; about righteousness, because I am going to the Father, where you can see me no longer; and about judgment, because the prince of this world now stands condemned.

But when he, the Spirit of truth, comes, he will guide you into all the truth. He will not speak on his own; he will speak only what he hears, and he will tell you what is yet to come. He will glorify me because it is from me that he will receive what he will make known to you

Then Jesus promised that the disciples would continue their travels in the company of the Holy Spirit. The Holy Spirit would be their Teacher, guiding them in good works, just as Jesus had done. The Spirit would not only shepherd their way, He would impel Jesus' teachings into action. Even though Jesus would not be present in the flesh, the disciples' ministry would stir the memory of Him, sharing His grace with the world. And so, the disciples realized that the Holy Spirit would fill their souls with grace. After a time of mourning, their tears would turn to joy.

John 17:6, 7-9, 11, 24
I have revealed you to those whom you gave me out of the world. They were yours; you gave them to me and they have obeyed your word. Now they know that everything you have given me comes from you. For I gave them the words you gave me and they accepted them. They knew with certainty that I came from you, and they believed that you sent me. I pray for them. I am not praying for the world, but for those you have given me, for they are yours.

I will remain in the world no longer, but they are still in the world, and I am coming to you. Holy Father, protect them by the power of your name, the name you gave me, so that they may be one as we are one.

Father, I want those you have given me to be with me where I am, and to see my glory, the glory you have given me because you loved me before the creation of the world.

Here, the deep love for His followers is exposed. Jesus could have complained to the Father about His disciples. He could have claimed that they'd failed to grasp His teachings concerning the cross that He had given them for over a year. He could have blamed Judas for His coming betrayal. He could have mocked the disciples for quarrelling about their greatness. He could have complained about their coming desertion of Him. Jesus did none of these things. He prayed to God on behalf of the disciples mentioning the good things they had done. So great was His love that each prayer to the Father was filled with thanks and adoration.

What truly magnificent things Jesus prayed for His disciples—and for all of His believers! Initially, Jesus prayed that the disciples would know God and Himself. This is eternal life, to know God or experience God. This eternal life was a quality of life not a quantity. Let it be known: Everyone will live forever, yet not all people will enjoy the fellowship of God.

Four times, Jesus prayed for harmony among the disciples and all of His followers, granting them peace in His absence. Through repetition Jesus emphasizes the tremendous importance of Christians being united. Sadly, Jesus takes unity far more seriously than some of His followers. Twice Jesus prayed for the protection of His disciples. Although He had already warned them that they were to lose their lives for the ministry, Jesus sought from the Father spiritual safety for those the Father had given Him. He asked the Father to shield the disciples from temptation and evil.

Next, Jesus requested that His followers have joyful lives. There are many verses throughout the Old Testament that urge God's people to be glad in the Spirit. In Psalm 16:11 David says to God, "You will fill me with joy in Your presence with eternal pleasures at Your right hand." In this prayer, Jesus asked twice that the Father would forever envelop His followers in joy.

Jesus then called on the Father to make the disciples morally good, according to His teachings. Whatever other qualities God's people are to possess, they are meant to be holy. This distinguishes followers from non-believers. Teaching holiness and repentance for sin was a novelty in Jesus' lifetime. People during the biblical age rarely heard such things. At the time, the false gods of other cultures were often morally corrupt beings who accepted their subjects' evil deeds, so long as the people remained loyal. When the Hebrews came along, proclaiming the Word of God and demanding moral goodness, many people were shocked by the message of such a great and marvelous God.

Finally, Jesus asked the Father to reveal His greatness to His disciples. Jesus feared that His followers would be weakened by their separation from Him and He yearned to be reunited with them soon. The tenderness and unyielding concern of Jesus' prayers should hearten all His people. There is no greater evidence that we are loved by Christ. His love exceeds the reaches of our understanding. Jesus doesn't want to be separated from us in this life. He eagerly anticipates being reunited with us in Heaven. Throughout this prayer, Jesus goes back and forth in expressing the truth that the disciples belonged to the Father and were a gift of the Father to the Son. Again, through repetition, Jesus shows what is especially important to the Father and Himself. Jesus loves us because of the One Who gave us to Him. In other words we are precious because given to Christ by the Father.

Personal Reflections:

1. When washing the disciples' feet, Jesus told Peter, "You do not realize now what I am doing, but later you will understand." This is a great promise for us all. We are told to trust Jesus, even when we don't understand His works, for He is the One who loves endlessly (John 13:1), He is in control of all things (John 13:3), He is God (John 13:3) and He is interested in the smallest details, joys, and fears of our lives. Even when we don't fully understand the Lord's mysterious ways, Jesus is trustworthy. What things are you struggling to understand in your life? What might God's will be for you under these circumstances?

2. The fact that believers are the gift of the Father to the Son should be as meaningful to us as to our Savior. Most parents save small gifts their young children give them. The gift given may be of no value to the world, but it is precious to the parent because it is an expression of love by their child. What the Father gives the Son is of great importance to Jesus. Do you draw encouragement today from the truth you are a gift to the Savior? Is your heart warmed by the knowledge that Jesus holds you close as a precious treasure received from His beloved Father?

John 14:26; 16:33
But the Advocate, the Holy Spirit, whom the Father will send in my name, will teach you all things and will remind you of everything I have said to you

I have told you these things, so that in me you may have peace. In this world you will have trouble. But take heart! I have overcome the world.

3. We walk steadily on the path of life as the Holy Spirit guides our thoughts and actions. As we study the Scriptures, Jesus breathes life into the word so

that we may apply God's message to our daily lives. Sunday upon Sunday, as the preacher teaches the Scripture, we meet with God and are guided, reproved, corrected, built up, and above all, loved. We're brought into God's presence so our love for Jesus is strengthened through the Holy Spirit. As Jesus said of the Holy Spirit, "He will bring glory to me by taking from what is mine and making it known to you" (John 16:14); and "When the Counselor comes, whom I will send to you from the Father, the Spirit of truth who goes out from the Father, he will testify about me" (John 15:26). Where can you see the Holy Spirit moving and working in your life? Where can you see the Holy Spirit in the lives of those around you? What is the Spirit teaching you today?

4. In John 17, Jesus teaches His followers what to pray and how to pray. He taught them to ask for unity with others, as well as harmony, protection from the evil one, a soul purified by the truth, and the courage to teach as Jesus taught and to love as God loves. If we meditate on Jesus' teachings at the Last Supper, our hearts may be opened to the compassion and security of His love. Jesus sought to spread peace in a troubled world. This was the purpose of the teachings: to fill His disciples with courage. When we follow His teachings, we too will inherit a confident spirit. Do your prayer requests resemble the prayers that Jesus spoke for His disciples? If not, what changes do you need to make?

Chapter 2

IN THE GARDEN

Matthew 26:30
When they had sung a hymn, they went out to the Mount of Olives.

The disciples and Jesus finished their Passover meal in the upper room. They left the house and walked through Jerusalem. Passing through the eastern gate of the city, they descended into the Kidron Valley and climbed the other side to the Mount of Olives. The Mount of Olives is a ridge east of Jerusalem where the Garden of Gethsemane is found. Jesus and the disciples would have passed by the campsites of countless pilgrims and seen the glowing embers from the evening fires that dotted the hillside. If it was a cloudless night, the full moon would have illuminated their path as they slowly threaded their way among the campers en route to the Garden of Gethsemane.

Mark 14:32-34
They went to a place called Gethsemane, and Jesus said to his disciples, "Sit here while I pray." He took Peter, James and John along with him, and he began to be deeply distressed and troubled. "My soul is overwhelmed with sorrow to the point of death," he said to them. "Stay here and keep watch."

Jesus had led the disciples to the Garden of Gethsemane for prayer many times before. On such an important occasion as Passover, the disciples would've expected Jesus to usher them once more to His beloved sanctuary. Gazing at the marble temple walls towering over the city walls, Jesus prayed for the wicked city, His mission, and His group of followers. Bathed in moonlight, Jerusalem was a spectacular site from the Garden.

Aside: Gethsemane means "oil press," and fittingly, the Garden of Gethsemane was an olive grove (John 18:1). It was also Jesus and the disciples' customary place of worship. Safely outside the city walls and away from crowds, the Garden provided sanctuary for Jesus' prayers and teachings.

On this evening, Jesus left eight of the disciples near the Garden entrance. Then He went inside with His closest and most beloved disciples, Peter, James and John and began sharing His sorrow with them. He'd never revealed His feelings about His upcoming persecution before. At this time, however, Jesus found it important to voice His sorrow.

Speaking to the disciples with such frank honesty both startled and unnerved His confidants. Jesus had calmed a storm with a single utterance, commanded the blind to see and the dead to rise. How could He suddenly feel fear? The disciples didn't know what to say or do to relieve His grief.

Matthew 26: 39

Going a little farther, he fell with his face to the ground and prayed, "My Father, if it is possible, may this cup be taken from me. Yet not as I will, but as you will

Luke 22:43-44

An angel from heaven appeared to him and strengthened him. And being in anguish, he prayed more earnestly, and his sweat was like drops of blood falling to the ground.

Having left the three remaining disciples, Jesus moved even farther into the Garden to be alone with God. Although the eleven disciples could hear Jesus' agonizing prayers, they simply couldn't fathom what He was about to endure. Jesus had taught them about the coming events of His crucifixion but they hadn't comprehended it's significance over the course of the year. In His solitude, Jesus pled with His Father for strength and comfort.

The prayer Jesus had spoken en route to the Garden (John 17), a request for the faith and protection of His disciples, was far removed from the prayers He uttered in the Garden of Gethsemane. Jesus' initial prayer had seemed gentle; even comforting. But His tranquility vanished once He faced the prospect of His own excruciating death. Alone and in anguish, Jesus called out, "Father if it is possible let this cup pass from me."

Jesus faced His greatest inner struggle in Gethsemane. Rephrased in modern terms, Jesus felt such distress that He said the situation was killing Him (Matthew 26:38). Matthew and Mark mentioned that their Master appeared to be "*perilypos*," meaning "deeply grieved" in Greek. So physically exhausting was the Lord's agony that the extreme exertion caused what Luke 22:44 records: "And His sweat was like drops of blood falling to the ground." It took all of the Savior's faith to carry on. Then an angel of God appeared, comforting Him and revitalizing His strength.

In truth, the thought of death didn't overwhelm Jesus, nor did the idea of the cruel physical suffering that He was to endure on the cross. Rather, it was the horrifying punishment of a tainted soul, the price of humankind's sin, which Jesus would absolve with His own purity. Jesus hadn't experienced sin, yet the sins of the world were about to be placed upon Him (1 John 2:2).

The condemnation awaiting Jesus would completely separate Him from God. It was this separation that grieved Him so deeply. Many times, Jesus had stated that He always pleased the Father (John 8:29). Jesus also delighted in saying, "I and the Father are one" (John 10:30). A perfect harmony existed between Jesus and God, and nothing before had interrupted Their pleasure and delight in one another.

Being subjected to the wrathful punishment of sin seemed unthinkable. Jesus was to endure for a time what lost souls will embrace for an eternity. He would assume the hell merited by our sins; offering His soul so that we might be delivered from such punishment. It was during this contemplation that God sent an angel to appear before Him. This was God's only recorded act of mercy towards Jesus as He prayed in the Garden. Jesus continued to pray with such intensity that sweat fell from Him like great drops of blood.

Then, vowing to the Father, "Not as I will but as you will," Jesus submitted Himself wholly to His Father's plan. The Savior knew that He must be sacrificed for the sake of humankind. At once, Jesus became calm and reposed. It was His destiny to die, and He would do so with unconditional love for all humanity. Jesus rose from prayer to calmly meet God's anger against sin. He would succeed—the battle was over, the victory won. Time and time again in the next few hours Jesus would overcome by the Spirit. Soon, everyone would know the name of Jesus and the calm courage He exhibited until He dismissed His spirit on the cross.

During the events that follow, we'll observe Jesus' divine conduct. Time and again, Jesus would overcome His enemies by spiritual rather than physical strength. Being taken captive, He would take captive His captors with His calm and majestic manner. They would be confused, frustrated, or angered by the gentle grace of this strange prisoner who refused to be afraid.

Mark 14: 37-41

Then he returned to his disciples and found them sleeping. "Simon," he said to Peter, "are you asleep? Couldn't you keep watch for one hour? Watch and pray so that you will not fall into temptation. The spirit is willing, but the flesh is weak." Once more he went away and prayed the same thing. When he came back, he again found them sleeping, because their eyes were heavy. They did not know what to say to him. Returning the third time, he said to them, "Are you still sleeping and resting? Enough! The hour has come. Look, the Son of Man is delivered into the hands of sinners.

While Jesus prayed, He asked the disciples Peter, James, and John to pray with Him, instead they fell asleep three separate times. As Jesus' closest followers, the trio comprised the inner circle of the twelve apostles. All three were offered special privileges but with privilege came responsibility. Jesus expected Peter, James, and John to take His request more seriously than the other disciples would. For this reason, He'd brought them deeper into the Garden than the other eight, charging them with the responsibility of praying for Him and with Him. This explains why His disappointment in them was so great.

Personal Reflections:

1. When we bare our soul in distressing situations, we tend to limit our circle of listeners. Jesus did this by voicing His sorrow to His closest

disciples. It's always a challenge deciding whether to speak up or suffer alone. Have you ever bared your soul to the wrong person? What did you learn from that experience? When have you bared your soul to the right person? How did these two situations compare?

2. No one feels more alone than a person who is emotionally abandoned, as Jesus was by His disciples. When they failed Him, He turned to His Father. When your friends have misunderstood you or failed you in another way, to whom did you turn? Did you seek God's help? Why or why not?

3. When people experience extraordinary pain, they often withdraw from others and share very few emotions. However, sharing pain with others helps to relieve a great burden, especially when it's entrusted to a truly compassionate and loving confidant. When have you shared your pain with others? Did you feel relief in doing so? Have you ever written about your suffering? If so, how was it helpful?

4. Solitude is a foreign thing to many people. Modern society is accustomed to "background noise," which masks the silence in our lives. People stroll through the park talking on cell phones; we go to sleep listening to music; hours a day are spent watching television. We feel a desperate need to be distracted by something. What do you need to do in order to meet with God in solitude? Do you need to go for a walk? Do you need to attend a retreat? How can you leave the background noise behind?

5. "Submission" has a very negative connotation in the present day. We feel the need to be in control at all times. If something is painful, we attempt to control it with drugs, blame, or evasion, instead of working to resolve it. Surrendering that struggle for dominance is frightening and difficult, even when we're forced to relinquish it. When was the last time you submitted to the will of God? How did you feel afterwards? Did you submit willingly? Why or why not?

6. If we're going to submit to the Father as Jesus did in the Garden of Gethsemane, we must trust in Him. What stands in the way of you trusting God enough to submit to His will?

7. Romans 10:17 states, "Faith comes from hearing the message, and the

message is heard through the Word of God." That is, in order to trust in God enough to submit to Him, we must feed on His Word. How consistently do you immerse yourself in the Bible?

8. As we pray during a particularly difficult time, our perspective on a situation may change. The thing we initially struggled with may seem less threatening. Through prayer, we learn to view situations as God sees them. As we say that prayer changes things, we may also say that prayer changes us. How diligent are you in prayer? How has prayer changed you?

Chapter 3

THE ARREST

John 11:47-50
Then the chief priests and the Pharisees called a meeting of the
Sanhedrin. "What are we accomplishing?" they asked. "Here is
this man performing many signs. If we let him go on like this,
everyone will believe in him, and then the Romans will come and
take away both our temple and our nation." Then one of them,
named Caiaphas, who was high priest that year, spoke up, "You
know nothing at all! You do not realize that it is better for you
that one man die for the people than that the whole nation perish

There were two powerful groups that aligned themselves against Jesus:
the Pharisees and the Sadducees. The Pharisees were teachers of Jewish
law: the Torah. In Jesus' day, roughly six-thousand of these teachers
were scattered throughout Israel, speaking about the Old Testament, the
immortality of the soul, and the afterlife. The Pharisees held authority
over the synagogues, the places of worship where the Torah was read
every Sabbath. They were incredibly strict with the Jewish people in their
interpretation of the law, particularly in regard to observing the Sabbath.
For example, if a man dragged his chair along a dirt floor, and the leg of the
chair made a furrow in the dirt, this was considered work, i.e. plowing. So,
the man had violated the law against working on the Sabbath by "plowing"
the dirt on the floor of his home. The Pharisees even debated allowing
their people to eat an egg laid by a hen on the Sabbath as she "labored" to
produce the egg thus violating the commandment to rest on the Sabbath.

In contrast, the Sadducees lived mostly in Jerusalem. These men controlled
the temple in Jerusalem where animal sacrifices took place every morning
and evening. The Sadducees were led by a high priest, a position of power
that rotated to a new priest every year. These leaders were rich, aristocratic,
and perceived as arrogant by the common people. The Sadducees believed
only in the five books of Moses (Genesis – Deuteronomy) and largely

ignored the rest of the Old Testament. Also, they denied the existence of the afterlife, angels, and the resurrection of the dead.

These two groups coexisted only in Jewish government. The government, known as the Sanhedrin, was composed of seventy-one members, a majority of whom were Sadducees. The Sanhedrin was led by the high priest and convened in Jerusalem when necessary.

Outside of the Sanhedrin, the Pharisees and the Sadducees had little to do with one another. However, they did unite due to their common hatred of Jesus. Jesus had turned many Jews against the Pharisees by proving that the Pharisees' interpretation of Jewish law was flawed. At the same time, Jesus had also threatened the authority of the Sadducees. Because He'd greatly jeopardized the power of both groups, they resolved to kill Him for the sake of the external unity of the Jewish nation.

Matthew 26:14-16
Then one of the Twelve—the one called Judas Iscariot—went to the chief priests and asked, "What are you willing to give me if I deliver him over to you?" So they counted out for him thirty pieces of silver. From then on Judas watched for an opportunity to hand him over

As mentioned, Judas had left Jesus and the other disciples midway through the Passover meal when Satan entered him (John 13:27-30). The previous Tuesday night, Judas had bargained with the high priests over the price and occasion when he would betray Jesus. He agreed to thirty pieces of silver, which Moses taught was the amount paid to an owner who had lost a slave (Exodus 21:32). It may seem strange that Judas didn't demand more from the priests. He easily could have bargained for a greater reward for such an important enemy. Given this fact, greed was not likely Judas' sole, or even primary motive that night.

What, then, was Judas' incentive for offering Jesus to His enemies? Like many who knew Jesus and considered Him the Messiah, Judas may have wanted Jesus to use His great power to overthrow the Romans. With their defeat, Christians would be free to begin a new kingdom of God, an earthly kingdom in which Judas, like the other apostles desired a special place. That very night, the disciples had fought over who would be first in the kingdom (Luke 22:24). Judas may have hoped to earn the favored place at Jesus' side by enabling Jesus to rise to power. If Jesus were captured and threatened with death, surely He would defend Himself against the Romans with His amazing power and usher in the kingdom.

Upon leaving the Passover meal, Judas hastened to the priests, declaring that he soon would betray Jesus. Judas hadn't planned to act on that particular night but Jesus had spoken to him in the upper room, telling him, "What you are about to do, do quickly" (John 13:27). It's possible that Judas was startled by Jesus' knowledge of the betrayal, so he went immediately to the high priests to uphold his part of plan.

Upon seeing the opportunity to capture Jesus on that Passover night, the high priest, Caiaphas, went quickly before Pilate, who was the Roman ruler of Palestine. Only the high priest could demand an audience with Pilate at such a late hour. Caiaphas requested that some of Pilate's men accompany the Jewish officials to arrest a dangerous man inside the city. Pilate obliged the high priest and sent nearly five hundred Roman troops to arrest Jesus (John 18:3).

There was a well-nursed hatred between Pilate and the Jews; however, Roman law mandated that a Roman ruler oversee all criminal cases that called for a death sentence. According to the law, Pilate reserved the right to approve the ruling of the Sanhedrin or, if he saw fit, reverse it. Pilate was bound by this law to oversee the coming trial and administer the ultimate punishment to Jesus if he deemed it appropriate.

John 18:2-3
Now Judas, who betrayed him, knew the place, because Jesus had often met there with his disciples. So Judas came to the garden, guiding a detachment of soldiers and some officials from the chief priests and the Pharisees. They were carrying torches, lanterns and weapons.

Judas likely led the priests and Roman troops to the house where Jesus and the disciples had shared the Passover meal. When the looming mob discovered that their culprit had gone, Judas knew precisely where to find

Jesus. He quickly led the troops toward the Garden of Gethsemane. During the three and one-half years that Judas had walked with Jesus, they'd often conducted prayer in this place, especially in times of great importance (Luke 22:39; John 18:2). Judas was certain that he would find Jesus there in the Garden.

Mark 14:44-45
Now the betrayer had arranged a signal with them: "The one I kiss is the man; arrest him and lead him away under guard." Going at once to Jesus, Judas said, "Rabbi!" and kissed him.

Matthew 26:50
Jesus replied, "Do what you came for, friend." Then the men stepped forward, seized Jesus and arrested him

Judas led the hostile group out of the city and towards the Garden of Gethsemane. The eight disciples waiting near the entrance undoubtedly saw the mob approaching. There were many Romans, and they carried torches. The soldiers' sandals with nail-studded soles crunched on the limestone path that led to Gethsemane. The eight disciples wondered who was coming and for what reason. Was this how Jesus was to be betrayed?

The Pharisees, the strictest of the Jewish leaders, marched beside the Roman soldiers who were armed with swords and staves and lanterns. It was no secret that the Jews and the Romans hated one another, particularly the Jewish leaders who were forced to submit to Roman law. Still, they must have hated Jesus much more, for the priests reveled in the pending arrest of the Savior, and were pleased to have the Roman soldiers among them.

The Jewish leaders hurried through the night to capture Jesus and unleash their harsh proceedings. He was popular with the common folk, which is why it was so critical that He be taken into Roman custody quickly. The priests wanted to ensure the prosecution was settled before the news of Jesus' arrest spread.

Judas planned to identify the "one they were to seize" by greeting Him with a kiss. A kiss was a sign of a student's devotion to his rabbi. The Greek term used in the text, "*katafalacen*," indicates excessive and repeated kisses from Judas (Matthew 26:49). We now understand that Judas feigned his love for Jesus.

Often overlooked, an unsettling detail in Judas' betrayal, is that Jesus called Judas "friend" after being kissed by him (Matthew 26:50) and in spite of being arrested. Jesus' love may have overpowered the betrayer and made Judas pause and question his deed perhaps for the first time.

The soldiers who came to arrest Jesus expected Him to do one of two things: flee or fight. The troops carried lanterns and torches in case He ran, as well as staves and swords in case He and His followers resisted. Despite all their precautions, the Romans weren't prepared for Jesus' actual response—surrender.

John 18:4-8

Jesus, knowing all that was going to happen to him, went out and asked them, "Who is it you want?" "Jesus of Nazareth," they replied. "I am he," Jesus said. (And Judas the traitor was standing there with them.) When Jesus said, "I am he," they drew back and fell to the ground. Again he asked them, "Who is it you want?" "Jesus of Nazareth," they said. Jesus answered, "I told you that I am he. If you are looking for me, then let these men go.

In light of the circumstances, Jesus' composure and compliance were contradictory, which is why the soldiers were caught off guard. He confronted the Roman troops and asked who they wanted rather than making physical threats. He also came forward to meet the mob peacefully.

When the soldiers asked whether He was Jesus of Nazareth, He responded: "I am." This shocked them since "I am" was also a way of saying "God" (Exodus 3:14). By replying this way, Jesus answered the question and proclaimed His real identity to the Romans. The crowd likely understood it as a confession of deity because they fell back with apparent humility and fear.

The soldiers soon regained their composure. Jesus asked them a second time whom they wanted. He assured the soldiers that He'd accompany them peacefully but His followers were to be set free. Even as He submitted to the soldiers' authority, He exercised authority over them by demanding his disciples' release.

Aside: Earlier that night, the disciples had bragged about their spiritual strength. Peter had even assured Jesus that he would follow Him to death. Jesus knew that the disciples were not to be arrested, jailed, or martyred at that time. As He was being arrested, He ensured the disciples' safety and spared them from His own punishment. This was His hour, their hour would come some years later.

Luke 22:49-51

When Jesus' followers saw what was going to happen, they said, "Lord, should we strike with our swords?" And one of them struck the servant of the high priest, cutting off his right ear. But Jesus answered, "No more of this!" And he touched the man's ear and healed him.

Just before the soldiers put their hands on Jesus, one of the disciples asked if he and the others should attack with their swords. Simon Peter brandished his weapon and leapt out to protect Jesus (John 18:10-11). The sword struck Malchus, a servant of the high priest, cutting off his right ear. Jesus healed it in a swift and pivotal act. He commanded Peter to put away his sword, saying, "Do you think I cannot call on my Father, and He will at once put at my disposal more than twelve legions of angels?" (Matthew 26:53). The disciples then realized that although they were terrified, they weren't supposed to protect Jesus from the Romans. His capture and arrest were necessary to fulfill God's plan.

Luke 22:52-53

Then Jesus said to the chief priests, the officers of the temple guard, and the elders, who had come for him, "Am I leading a rebellion, that you have come with swords and clubs? Every day I was with you in the temple courts, and you did not lay a hand on me. But this is your hour—when darkness reigns."

Having spared His disciples and healed the servant Malchus, Jesus released verbal judgment on the mob. He hadn't acted as a threat to anyone and was neither armed nor dangerous. He had taught in public, side by side with the priests in Jerusalem. The measures the high priests had orchestrated to arrest this compassionate and holy man were both ludicrous and extreme.

Jesus continued, "But this is your hour—when darkness reigns" (Luke 22:53). As the darkness of sin was engulfing His captors, Jesus assured them indirectly, "My hour is coming."

John 18:12
Then the detachment of soldiers with its commander and the
Jewish officials arrested Jesus. They bound him

Mark 14:50-51
Then everyone deserted him and fled. A young man, wearing
nothing but a linen garment, was following Jesus. When they seized
him,

Jesus was arrested, and His followers deserted Him. Yet as the soldiers led Him away, they noticed a young man following them closely. It's thought by some scholars that this was John Mark, author of the Gospel of Mark, although he was not a disciple of Jesus at that time. One of the soldiers lunged at the boy, grasping only his linen robe as he fled. Although the soldiers freed the disciples at Jesus' command, they trusted no witness of the events at Gethsemane. No one, including a naked young man, should complicate Jesus' arrest. However the young man made good his escape. Then, Jesus was led from the Garden to the high priest's home to stand trial.

Personal Reflections:

1. The Garden of Gethsemane was a sanctuary for Jesus. Knowing this, Satan sought to destroy Him in this sacred place. In the same way, Satan seeks to interrupt our prayers, worship, and fellowship with other Christians and the Lord. Do you have a prayer sanctuary? How do you remain focused in prayer? Is your prayer time a source of strength? Do you sometimes feel distracted from your time with God?

2. Jesus' betrayal was especially bitter because Judas was a friend. As it says in Psalm 55:12-14:

> If an enemy were insulting me, I could endure it; if a foe were rising against me, I could hide. But it is you, a man like myself, my companion, my close friend, with whom I once enjoyed sweet fellowship at the house of God, as we walked about among the worshipers.

By calling Judas His friend after being betrayed by him, Jesus showed us how to behave when we're wronged by someone dear to us. Jesus said to respond with love and grace, speak kindly to them and be slow to anger (Matthew 5:44). A calm and gentle response may be the key to rectifying a bad situation. How have you responded to a friend's betrayal? Were you quick to anger? If so, how might you have responded differently in the situation?

3. If Jesus calls Judas "friend," imagine how he feels about us, the ones who seek to faithfully follow Him. Whatever sins we may have committed, Jesus desires a close and loving relationship with each of us. He doesn't hold grudges, nor does He distance Himself from us. When we come before God to confess our failures, we receive a joyous reception (Luke 15:17-24). Have you ever hesitated to approach Him? Why were you uncertain? Were your uncertainties justified?

4. The same Jesus who shielded His disciples from the mob is watching over you today. Jesus is the Good Shepherd. He won't allow anything to harm us without providing the necessary guidance and comfort so that we may bear it (1 Corinthians 10:13). Are you prepared to let the Good Shepherd guide you throughout your life? Do you trust that He will amply prepare the way for you? Why or why not?

Chapter 4

JESUS BEFORE ANNAS

John 18: 12-14

Then the detachment of soldiers with its commander and the Jewish officials arrested Jesus. They bound him and brought him first to Annas, who was the father-in-law of Caiaphas, the high priest that year. Caiaphas was the one who had advised the Jewish leaders that it would be good if one man died for the people.

Despite the high priest's sense of urgency, the operation had gone smoothly. The Roman soldiers must have laughed among themselves at how easily they'd arrested Jesus. Following the Jewish officials' directions, the arresting officers had marched back into the city with their prisoner. They didn't realize that the night wouldn't conclude as quickly.

Although Caiaphas was the official high priest at the time, and therefore the official head of the Sadducees, Annas held the ultimate authority over the Jews. Annas had been high priest from about 6 A.D. until 15 A.D. However, he'd offended the Romans by imposing and executing capital sentences without Roman approval, decisions that were outside his jurisdiction. As a result, he'd been deposed by the Roman governor, Valerius Gratus. Despite his removal from office, the Jewish people considered Annas to be the true high priest. Accordingly, in John 18:19, Annas is referred to as the high priest, and in John 18:13 and 24, Caiaphas is also called the high priest.

Annas was shrewd and crafty. After being deposed by the Romans, he manipulated the structure of authority and arranged for each of his five sons to take his position for a year. Thereafter, he made arrangements for his son-in-law, Caiaphas, to have the distinction. By bringing Jesus to Annas first, the Jewish officials were showing who the real power was behind the Jewish nation.

Annas was also first among those who yearned for Jesus' persecution. Jesus had cleansed the temple in Jerusalem, interrupting Sadducean business on the previous Monday (Mark 11:15-18). This was the second time He'd done this—John 2:13-22 records the first instance at the beginning of His ministry. Selling sacrificial animals in the temple had made Annas' family very wealthy but Jesus had powerfully reprimanded the people inside, calling them thieves and robbers. He posed a possible financial threat to the Sadducees and they took great offence at His bold actions. Little wonder then that Jesus' travails began with Annas.

Beyond wanting vengeance, the master manipulator feared and respected Jesus' extraordinary powers, including the raising of Lazarus, which Annas had heard about from Caiaphas. With the exception of two miracles, the cursing of the fig tree (Mark 11:12-21) and the annihilation of the herd of pigs (Luke 8:26-39), Jesus had only used His power out of compassion, such as healing the sick and restoring sight to the blind. But Annas and his followers didn't know this and likely feared that Jesus would turn His powers on them. The Sadducees realized that if He were free to continue His mission, all priests would be threatened. This self-appointed rabbi had to be stopped at all costs.

In their haste to condemn Jesus, the Sadducees abandoned propriety and adherence to law. Annas allowed a number of illegal actions during Jesus' preliminary hearing. In Jewish law, the court was required to convene to hear evidence offered by witnesses. Thereafter, officials would judge whether there was sufficient evidence to proceed to trial. The accused wasn't required to appear or defend himself at the initial hearing; he was considered innocent and not officially on trial until the court had given the authorities permission to proceed to trial. There was no reason to arrest Jesus prior to trial because He was still innocent according to Jewish law.

Another illegal aspect of the preliminary hearing was that it took place at night. Jewish law stated that court was not allowed to convene at night for a case related to a capital offence. What's more, a judge couldn't sit alone with the accused to interrogate him or judge his legal rights. This private and condemning examination Annas was conducting was expressly prohibited by Jewish law. Clearly, Jesus wasn't arrested to undergo a legal trial. The Jewish leaders had seized Him with the intention of getting rid of Him by any and all means. In other words the verdict was in before the trial happened.

John 18: 19-21

Meanwhile, the high priest questioned Jesus about his disciples and his teaching. "I have spoken openly to the world," Jesus replied. "I always taught in synagogues or at the temple, where all the Jews come together. I said nothing in secret. Why question me? Ask those who heard me. Surely they know what I said.

Annas demanded two things from Jesus: a list of His followers and a statement of His teachings and beliefs. Annas showed his ignorance here. As the revered, de facto leader of the Jewish people, he was the head of the temple and supposed to know what was going on within his religious jurisdiction. He should have known the information he was asking for from Jesus.

In response to the first of Annas' demands, Jesus flatly refused to divulge the names of His followers and friends so He ignored that question.

Responding to the second demand for information about His teachings, Jesus clarified that He wasn't teaching anything subversively. Everything was conducted in public; nothing was ever said in secret. In Luke 6:6-11, Scripture tells us that Jesus taught in the synagogue and healed a man's withered hand in the presence of the scribes and Pharisees. At the time, the Pharisees said and did nothing. Jesus' answer not only reaffirmed what the Jewish leaders knew to be true, He also emphasized that he wasn't meeting in secret—unlike the officials who were convening His trial out of the public eye. Jesus clearly implied "I only do business in the public arena and not behind closed doors like you do." Annas had been soundly rebuked. Again we see how Jesus controlled the situation.

Jesus refused to tell Annas about the content of His teachings. Instead, Jesus advised him to go out to the temple or synagogues and ask anyone there what He taught. All those who frequented the religious establishments Annas ruled could easily recite Jesus' teachings. This was another important rebuke against Annas: Common men, with little societal responsibility and no authority over the temple, knew much more than Annas about what was being taught there.

By mentioning followers, Jesus was also reminding Annas that witnesses were needed to testify against Him. The commoners who studied with Him at the temple wouldn't comply. In order for the officials to begin Jesus' persecution, witnesses had to be united against Him and their testimony had to agree. Annas had no right to question Jesus on His conduct and supporters. Jesus was clearly correcting Annas, and appealing to the protection of the Jewish law against the illegal—and soon to be brutal—treatment He was receiving. This is the first of several challenges Jesus would put to His accusers. He continually called on them to be aware of their actions and reconsider the crimes they were committing.

John 18: 22-23
When Jesus said this, one of the officials nearby slapped him in the face. "Is this the way you answer the high priest?" he demanded. "If I said something wrong," Jesus replied, "testify as to what is wrong. But if I spoke the truth, why did you strike me?

A guard dealt Jesus a blow to the face and charged Him, "Do you answer the high priest so?" (John 18:22). This act of brutality wasn't acceptable in Jewish society. In most instances, its legal system afforded the accused every consideration until a ruling had been decided, especially in a capital case. Jesus was summarily stripped of such considerations.

It's interesting that when Jesus was struck by the guard, He didn't turn the other cheek as He had counselled His disciples to do (Matthew 5:40). Many other illegal acts occurred that night under the guise of the administration of justice yet Jesus remained silent. At this point, however, He reminded his opponents of His rights and named the situation for what it was: a farce. Annas was nevertheless satisfied with the findings of his informal hearing and decided that enough evidence had been gathered. He then sent Jesus to Caiaphas, bound and destined to stand a full trial.

Personal Reflections:

1. Sometimes it's difficult to speak up against injustice. It may be easier just to remain silent, although many innocent people are naturally defensive and vocal on their own behalf. Jesus' preliminary hearing demonstrates that while we must attest to injustice, sometimes it's so evident that it speaks for itself. Often, we need to watch for the proper time and manner to stand up for our rights.

This is a hard concept to internalize, and even more difficult to put into practice. When situations go awry and people act unjustly, we feel compelled to rectify the wrongs. We wish to assume the role of defenders of truth. However, what is good and truthful rarely needs a champion. The truth can and often does stand up for itself. In the long run, truth will always triumph.

Think of a time when you wanted to fight an injustice that had been committed against you. Did you? If so, what happened? If not, why did you choose to remain silent? Were you happy with your decision?

2. When we're being treated unfairly, it may be difficult to turn the other cheek and remain vulnerable to those who are mistreating us. Think of a time when you had the opportunity to turn the other cheek. Did you? Why or why not?

3. When people are losing an argument, they often resort to shouting. They hope to intimidate when they can't otherwise win the dispute. It is an effort to make up in violence for what is lacking in substance. This is called "winning through intimidation" and it often works. When you're in a dispute and it appears that the other person is prevailing, do you find yourself resorting to intimidation? Is winning more important than discovering the truth? Is discovering the truth more important than being right or wrong?

4. Jesus showed remarkable patience towards those who persecuted Him, enduring the injustice in silence. If Jesus is this patient towards those who hate Him, how patient is He towards those who love Him? How patient is He towards those who love Him but fail Him? What does this mean for

you when you come to Him seeking forgiveness for your failures?

Chapter 5

JESUS BEFORE THE SANHEDRIM

Matthew 26: 59-68

The chief priests and the whole Sanhedrin were looking for false evidence against Jesus so that they could put him to death. But they did not find any, though many false witnesses came forward. Finally two came forward and declared, "This fellow said, 'I am able to destroy the temple of God and rebuild it in three days.' " Then the high priest stood up and said to Jesus, "Are you not going to answer? What is this testimony that these men are bringing against you?" But Jesus remained silent. The high priest said to him, "I charge you under oath by the living God: Tell us if you are the Messiah, the Son of God." "You have said so," Jesus replied. "But I say to all of you: From now on you will see the Son of Man sitting at the right hand of the Mighty One and coming on the clouds of heaven." Then the high priest tore his clothes and said, "He has spoken blasphemy! Why do we need any more witnesses? Look, now you have heard the blasphemy. What do you think?" "He is worthy of death," they answered. Then they spit in his face and struck him with their fists. Others slapped him and said, "Prophesy to us, Messiah. Who hit you?"

After the preliminary trial before Annas, Jesus was brought before Caiaphas and the Sanhedrin. This was the second part of the first trial that Jesus was to undergo the night of His betrayal. The first trial was held before the Jewish religious leaders, which consisted of three separate proceedings: a preliminary trial before Annas (John 18:13-24), which we've already discussed; a main trial before the Sanhedrin (Mark 14:53, 55-65; Matthew 26:57, 59-68; Luke 22:54, 63-65; John 18:24); and an additional main trial before the Sanhedrin that occurred after dawn (Mark 15:1; Matthew 27:1; Luke 22:66-71).

The second and final trial was conducted before the Romans. Caiaphas, the high priest in the eyes of the Romans, was the main perpetrator during the final stages of the Jewish trial proceedings. The demeanor of Caiaphas and the other Jewish leaders throughout those events starkly contrasted with the composure of Jesus. On one hand, the Sanhedrin acted with dishonor, cowardice, and incredible baseness. Jesus, on the other hand, maintained His dignity in addition to His calm spirit. There are various explanations for Jesus' peaceful demeanor when all else was driven by chaos and evil. The explanation that best fits the gospel description is that Jesus was ultimately in control of His own destiny. His betrayal and now His persecution were transpiring as they needed to unfold, and therefore Jesus allowed the events to continue.

In about 200 A.D., Rabbi Judah recounted to writing what had been to that time the established practice of the administration of justice in the law courts of Israel. The new legal text, which captured and codified the established practice, became known as the Mishnah. The Mishnah clearly described the ways and means of due process in criminal prosecutions. In regard to capital cases, Jewish law mandated that the court had to reach a clear majority on the verdict. If a majority was established, the court then had to wait twenty-four hours to reconvene for a second vote. During the second vote, no one could change from voting not guilty to voting guilty. Only those who had previously voted guilty could change their decision. After the second vote, the sentence could be passed. A trial that proceeded in this manner was considered to be extremely fair. Jesus' trial, however, did not proceed in this fashion.

To reiterate, the law specified that capital trials must be conducted during daylight hours; Jesus' trial was held at night. A clear charge for the offence must be brought against the accused at the outset of the trial, yet the Jewish leaders did not initially have a charge against Jesus. They simply maintained that whatever He'd done must warrant the most severe penalty: death. The suspect needed to be properly arraigned, or brought before the court to answer the charges against him. In Jesus' case, multiple trial proceedings were conducted immediately. Other illegalities included: a lack of preparation time for defense prior to the trial, false witnesses, and forcing the accused to testify against Himself under oath.

The final requirement for a fair trial under Jewish law was the harmonious testimonies of two or more witnesses to the alleged crime. The Jewish leaders found it challenging to meet this requirement. As Jesus' trial progressed, many witnesses came forward but none of their false testimonies were in agreement—not until the last two people spoke. These witnesses testified that Jesus had prophesied that He could rebuild the temple in three days. When Caiaphas asked Jesus directly, "What is this they testify against you?" (Mark 14:60) Jesus made no comment. Jewish law said He could remain silent and was not to be coerced into testifying against Himself.

Caiaphas saw his opportunity to destroy Jesus slipping away and promptly put Jesus under oath to testify against Himself; asking if He was the Christ, the Son of God. Now, if Jesus had maintained His silence, it would have be a denial of His Father. Thus, Jesus was required to speak rather than contradict all that He had taught.

Jesus' answer was an unequivocal "Yes!" (Matthew 26:64). In that moment, all pretense of a civilized trial was discarded. The Sanhedrin understood Jesus' answer meant, yes, He was the Son of God and that He would sit at the right hand of God in a position of righteousness. Such a claim to deity was blasphemy, which was a capital offence under Jewish law (Leviticus 24:16). Had Jesus claimed to be the Messiah, according to the Jewish expectation of a Messiah, He would not have necessarily been claiming to be God's Son. The Jewish expectation of a Messiah was for the establishment of an earthly kingdom, not a heavenly one. With Jesus' claim to deity, the Sanhedrin had all the evidence it needed to convict Jesus of a crime punishable by death (assuming Jesus lied).

Once he was convicted, Jesus' guards became physically violent against Him. Blindfolding Him, they took turns abusing Him, bowing to Him in mockery and pestering Him to prophesy which guard had hit Him. One spat in His face and asked what His name was. Others struck Jesus again and again. This abuse continued until the guards grew tired of performing indignities on their silent victim (Matthew 26:67-68; Mark 14:65; Luke 22:67-68 cf. Isaiah 53:7).

John 18:15-16
Simon Peter and another disciple were following Jesus. Because this disciple was known to the high priest, he went with Jesus into

the high priest's courtyard, but Peter had to wait outside at the door. The other disciple, who was known to the high priest, came back, spoke to the servant girl on duty there and brought Peter in.

Mark 14:66-68
While Peter was below in the courtyard, one of the servant girls of the high priest came by. When she saw Peter warming himself, she looked closely at him. "You also were with that Nazarene, Jesus," she said. But he denied it. "I don't know or understand what you're talking about," he said, and went out into the entryway.

While Jesus suffered abuse from the Sanhedrin, Peter was struggling to face his own demons. His devotion to Jesus was initially honorable; he shadowed the group that led Jesus out of the Garden and back to Jerusalem. Peter truly loved Jesus and hoped that He would demonstrate His marvelous power by liberating Himself. Peter had seen Jesus perform miraculous things. Since Jesus was the Son of God, surely He would do something to overturn what appeared to be defeat.

When the arresting crowd transferred Jesus from Annas' home to Caiaphas' home, where the Sanhedrin had assembled (Matthew 26:57-58), two of the disciples were following. Peter trailed behind at a distance (Mark 14:54). He was not permitted into the court, initially. A second disciple, who followed with Jesus (John 18:15) was known by the high priest and readily entered the court. The details about these events, which were recorded in the Gospel of John (John 18:12-16) suggest that it was John who appeared there. Once the house seemed safe, the second disciple spoke to the maid who kept the door and asked that Peter be admitted (John 18:16).

As Peter and the other disciple entered into the court, the maid attending the door looked at Peter and said, "You are one of His disciples, are you not?" (John 18:17). Peter quickly denied any connection with the accused and brushed by her, eager to get away from her questioning.

Matthew 26: 71-72
Then he went out to the gateway, where another servant girl saw him and said to the people there, "This fellow was with Jesus of

Nazareth." He denied it again, with an oath: "I don't know the man!"

The night was cold, and a fire had been lit in the middle of the courtyard to provide some warmth to the patrons. A group of minor officials and soldiers was huddled around it. Peter promptly joined them. From the fireside they could see and hear the proceedings before the Sanhedrin, as the courtyard allowed them to see into each room of the residence. In the dim light of the predawn with the firelight flickering across Peter's fear-strained face, a maid of the high priest studied him intently. Suddenly she spoke, boldly and condemningly. She exclaimed to the men around the fire, "This man was with Him!" (Luke 22:56). Terror struck Peter's heart, and he vigorously denied the charge for a second time.

Matthew 26: 73-75
After a little while, those standing there went up to Peter and said, "Surely you are one of them; your accent gives you away." Then he began to call down curses, and he swore to them, "I don't know the man!" Immediately a rooster crowed. Then Peter remembered the word Jesus had spoken: "Before the rooster crows, you will disown me three times." And he went outside and wept bitterly.

Luke 22: 61-62
The Lord turned and looked straight at Peter. Then Peter remembered the word the Lord had spoken to him: "Before the rooster crows today, you will disown me three times." And he went outside and wept bitterly.

Peter then joined in the conversation to dispel any further suspicion about his connection with Jesus. An hour later (Luke 22:59), one of those around the fire who had noticed Peter's Galilean accent, a man who was related to the one whom Peter had wounded in the garden, addressed him: "Didn't I see you with Him in the garden?" (John 18:26). "Surely you are one of them, your accent gives you away" (Matthew 26:73).

Then Peter was beside himself with fear. He began to cry out and swear that he knew nothing about the man claiming to be Christ. As he protested, everyone in the courtyard heard the cock crow. Peter was startled into silence. He remembered Jesus' words: "Before the rooster crows today, you will disown me three times." (Luke 22:61). Peter then noticed Jesus glancing at him, just for a moment.

What message would have been conveyed in that look? There was probably pain, as Jesus would have heard the cock crowing but there was no anger or bitterness. Had Jesus glared at Peter, the crowd would have known that its accusation against him was true. Instead, Jesus' eyes were filled with sorrow and compassion—sorrow that Peter had caved in the face of danger and compassion because of His ongoing love for him.

Elizabeth Barrett Browning wrote a poem entitled "The Meaning Of The Look", that seems to capture what may have gone through the Master's mind upon realizing that His prophecy of Peter's thrice denial had come true. It is a poem well worth including here.

The Meaning of the Look

I THINK that look of Christ might seem to say—
'Thou Peter! art thou then a common stone
Which I at last must break my heart upon,
For all God's charge to His high angels may
Guard my foot better? Did I yesterday
5
Wash *thy* feet, my beloved, that they should run
Quick to deny me 'neath the morning sun?
And do thy kisses, like the rest, betray?
The cock crows coldly.—Go, and manifest
A late contrition, but no bootless fear
10
For when thy final need is dreariest,
Thou shalt not be denied, as I am here;
My voice to God and angels shall attest,
Because I KNOW *this man, let him be clear.'*

Realizing what he'd done, Jesus' most adamant disciple was overcome with shame. He fled the scene weeping bitterly under the weight of his failure. In his anguish, Peter possibly didn't believe there was hope for reconciliation with His Master.

Matthew 27: 3-10

When Judas, who had betrayed him, saw that Jesus was condemned, he was seized with remorse and returned the thirty pieces of silver to the chief priests and the elders. "I have sinned," he said, "for I have betrayed innocent blood." "What is that to us?" they replied. "That's your responsibility." So Judas threw the money into the temple and left. Then he went away and hanged himself. The chief priests picked up the coins and said, "It is against the law to put this into the treasury, since it is blood money." So they decided to use the money to buy the potter's field as a burial place for foreigners. That is why it has been called the Field of Blood to this day. Then what was spoken by Jeremiah the prophet was fulfilled: "They took the thirty pieces of silver, the price set on him by the people of Israel, and they used them to buy the potter's field, as the Lord commanded me."

Like Peter, Judas was ashamed of himself. In spite of his successful betrayal of Jesus for personal gain, Judas wasn't out celebrating. He'd never intended his master to be crucified. As the night of persecution drew on, Judas recognized that Jesus wouldn't free Himself from the grip of the Jewish leaders or liberate the Jews from Roman rule using His God-given power. Instead, He was permitting Himself to be sacrificed. Things had gone terribly wrong.

After witnessing Jesus' condemnation, Judas repented to the chief priests and elders and wanted to refund the thirty pieces of silver to them. He confessed, "I have sinned, for I have betrayed innocent blood" (Matthew 27:4). The chief priests and elders turned on Judas. "What is that to us? That is your own iniquity" (Matthew 27:5). Having used Judas for their own evil purposes, the leaders now wanted nothing to do with him.

Then Judas, who had been standing just outside the temple, turned and threw the coins onto the floor and left. He lost all hope of ever reconciling with Christ and believed that the only course of action remaining was suicide. Judas went straight from the temple to the place where he hanged himself (Matthew 27:5; Acts 1:18, 19).

Both Peter and Judas had failed Jesus and repented for their actions. But Peter didn't take his life; instead, he acknowledged his shortcomings and asked for Jesus' mercy. Peter lived on to be reconciled with His Lord.

On the morning of Jesus' resurrection, the angel told the women at the tomb, "But go, tell his disciples and Peter, He is going ahead of you into Galilee. There you will see him, just as he told you" (Mark 16:7). Here, the specific mention of the disciple who'd denied Jesus three times showed reconciliation and forgiveness for his sins. Later on that same day, Jesus had a private audience with Peter, of which no detail was recorded (Luke 24:34). The same love and resolution would have been granted to Judas had he chosen to live on with remorse as Peter had done.

In 2 Corinthians 7:8-10, Paul speaks of two types of repentance: The first, Godly repentance, is where the sin is judged according to the will of God. Peter's repentance led him straight into God's forgiving arms. Peter had already determined that he needed Jesus at all costs (John 13:6-9) and now he wouldn't desert Him again.

The second kind of repentance is sorrow that leads ultimately to death. Judas, however remorseful he was, didn't repent to God. Instead, he confessed to the chief priests and elders who couldn't forgive his sins. It was a tragedy that Judas wouldn't turn to the One who actually could help him; the Friend of Sinners, the One who called him "friend," and the One who had shown him such love and privilege for several years. Judas' sorrow and turning away from God led him into a world of eternal darkness.

Luke 22:66-23:1

At daybreak the council of the elders of the people, both the chief priests and the teachers of the law, met together, and Jesus was led before them. "If you are the Messiah," they said, "tell us." Jesus answered, "If I tell you, you will not believe me, and if I asked you, you would not answer. But from now on, the Son of Man will be seated at the right hand of the mighty God." They all asked, "Are you then the Son of God?" He replied, "You say that I am." Then they said, "Why do we need any more testimony? We have heard it from his own lips. Then the whole assembly rose and led him off to Pilate.

This brief questioning before the Jewish religious leaders occurred immediately after dawn, giving the trial a façade of legality by placing it between sunrise and sunset. The required two trial sessions for a capital offence with a guilty verdict each time was also met, even though twenty-four hours hadn't elapsed between them. The Jewish leaders broke many laws of judicial conduct over the course of Jesus' trial, yet their misdeeds were disregarded. The second, or Roman trial also had three parts. First before Pilate (Mark 15:1-5; Matthew 27:2, 11-14; Luke 23:1-5; John 18:28-38) then before Herod (Luke 23:6-12), and then again before Pilate (Mark 15:6-15; Matthew 27:15-26; Luke 23:13-25; John 18:39-19:16). To execute Jesus, the Roman governor's approval was required.

Personal Reflections:

1. Those who remain calm in the midst of the storm, as Jesus did throughout His trial, provide an admirable example to others. Was Jesus calm because He was ignorant about what was going to happen? No. Did Jesus perceive His own guilt and maintain a sense of calm to trick others? No. Was Jesus calm because He didn't care about what was about to happen? No. Jesus was calm because He trusted God and knew that His Father was in control. In light of this, consider a difficult and emotionally taxing situation that you have experienced. What can you learn from Jesus' unrelenting trust in God in the face of great adversity? How can you apply these lessons to your situation?

2. The men conducting Jesus' trial, the Sanhedrin, occupied the upper echelon of Jewish society. Nevertheless, this select group participated in crude and inhumane actions as the trial progressed. Whenever a group of people participates in sinful behaviours, dehumanizing results seem to appear rapidly. We must be especially careful when sin presents itself in a crowd, a group, or an entire society. The safety of a crowd can easily result in "mob mentality," where those involved ignore their better judgment and slide into debasing activity. No human being is immune to mob mentality or public sin and nothing sanctions sin as readily as seeing others participate in it. Have you ever been in a situation where a crowd participated in ugly

behaviour? What did you do? What would you do differently if you were in the same situation again?

It's clear that the Sanhedrin condemned itself by committing a rapid succession of sins in its effort to prosecute and execute Jesus. We must learn to recognize sin so that we can repent for wrong behavior and return to God's grace right away. What are some things you can do to avoid committing one sin after another?

3. Jesus is a master in the art of reconciliation. In a single glance, He administers grace to Peter after Peter denies Him three times. In Scripture, we witness Jesus' understanding of the mortified disciple. Nothing is recorded of Peter's perspective regarding the resurrection (Luke 24:34). Instead, we see the continued intimacy and privacy of his reconciliation with his beloved Master. After their reunion, the restored Peter went on to become a pillar (Galatians 2:9) of the early church. Based on what we see of the unconditional bond between Peter and Christ, what can we infer about Christ's relationship with us? How does Christ see us when we fail Him?

4. At this point in history, many Jews longed for their own head of government. In keeping with this desire, the twelve disciples argued who would hold the greatest authority alongside Jesus in the coming kingdom (Matt. 20:20-21; Mark 9:34). Judas didn't want Jesus to die; on the contrary, his goal was to enable Jesus to become a political leader in order to liberate the Jews. Nevertheless, Judas' greater purpose in betraying Jesus failed. What does Judas' betrayal and subsequent suicide tell us about the greatness of Jesus' agenda versus our own? What happens when we try to use His power for our agendas?

5. There is great debate about what type of eternity awaits Christians who commit suicide. Some religious leaders believe that people who commit suicide are completely lost to God. Scripture, however, does not substantiate this notion. Suicide is a sin, but the Christian is not condemned to Hell by committing it. According to Romans 8:1-2, "Therefore, there is now no condemnation for those who are in Christ Jesus, because through Christ Jesus, the law of the Spirit of life set me free from the law of sin and death." This means that Christians, who commit any sin, including suicide, cannot

be condemned to hell for it. Instead, God will forgive them for it. Why do we tend to judge those who have committed suicide? Do we need to judge one another when we know that God is the ultimate judge of all?

Chapter 6

JESUS BEFORE PILATE

Matthew 27:11-14

Meanwhile Jesus stood before the governor, and the governor asked him, "Are you the king of the Jews?" "You have said so," Jesus replied. When he was accused by the chief priests and the elders, he gave no answer. Then Pilate asked him, "Don't you hear the testimony they are bringing against you?" But Jesus made no reply, not even to a single charge—to the great amazement of the governor.

For the Gentile trial, Jesus appeared before Pontius Pilate (Mark 15:1-5; Matthew 27:2, 11-14; Luke 23:1-5; John 18:28-38), then Herod (Luke 23:7-11), and then back to Pilate (Mark 15:6-15; Matthew 27:15-26: Luke 23:13-25; John 18:39-19:16). At the start, we meet the governor, Pilate, who was made procurator of Judea in 26 A.D. and survived in office until 36 A.D. His predecessor was Valerius Gratus, who had had many difficulties governing the Jewish nation, as well as the Samaritans. Pilate's immediate superior was Vitellius, the governor of Syria. Vitellius was the man who would eventually depose Pilate by sending him to Rome after one of his quarrels with the Samaritans.

Pilate neither understood nor cared to understand the unusual ways of the Jewish people. The Jews of Jesus' time were deliberately culturally unique from the surrounding groups. Jews kept to themselves wherever they lived; they customarily clustered around their house of prayer (a Synagogue) in a specific section of each city. Jews avoided public amusements. Their dietary laws did not permit them to eat with Gentiles. Jewish religious intolerance confused the Romans who were largely accepting of other gods. Jewish opposition to images of other gods, specifically in the form of idols and religious artifacts, caused many public controversies. Moreover, Jews were also seen fighting over religious issues amongst themselves. Overall, Jewish practices were an offence to many pagans of the time. As with most Gentiles, Pilate was offended by Jewish customs.

Pilate had several famous quarrels with the people he governed. The Romans accommodatingly deferred to the Jews' sensitivities about idols. When a governor and his troops entered Jerusalem, they always disassembled the legionary standards under which they had marched outside the city. The flags were put away and not reassembled until the troops left the city. However, one night, Pilate marched his soldiers into Jerusalem with their religious banners unfurled. When the Jews awoke the next morning and discovered that the holy city had been defiled by Pilate, there was a huge uproar. For almost a week, the Jews petitioned Pilate to remove the offensive flags. Pilate refused. When the complaints persisted, Pilate threatened to kill the Jews if they didn't abstain from quarreling. In response, the Jews laid bare their necks and insisted that they would rather die than see offensive emblems flying in their city. Pilate finally relinquished his stance and removed the offending banners. This scene occurred early in Pilate's reign, setting the tone for many such encounters with the Jews. Over time, the Jewish nation grew adept at prevailing in its arguments.

Later in his rule, Pilate raided the temple treasury to finance the aqueduct that he'd built along the Bethlehem road to Jerusalem. This was an even greater offence against the Jews. The situation came to a head when Pilate returned to Jerusalem shortly after the robbery. The time most likely coincided with the feast of the Passover, a time when many Jews migrated to Jerusalem for a celebration. As was his custom, Pilate was present for this special festival, accompanied by his best troops. Disguising some of his men as Jewish pilgrims, Pilate dispersed the soldiers among the crowds. When the disgruntled Jews broke out in a riot against Pilate's treachery, the soldiers began to beat the people. Contrary to orders, some soldiers drew their swords and spilled Jewish blood. Galileans were also present at the time of the riot, which may have been remembered by Luke who mentioned the "Galileans whose blood Pilate had mixed with their sacrifices" (Luke 13:1). In addition to outraging the Jewish population, this event would explain the animosity between Pilate and Herod Antipas, the ruler of the Galileans.

Yet another dispute between Pilate and the Jews involved the wooden shields mounted on his Jerusalem residence. He may have had them installed to help restore respect for his authority. When he didn't respond to their appeal to have the shields removed, the Jews appealed directly to Caesar, who instantly reprimanded Pilate. The emperor sympathized with the Jews and ordered the governor to remove the offensive items straightaway. Pilate had no choice but to comply with the Jews' request.

These conflicts set the stage for the most dramatic encounter of all: 'The trial of Jesus', an event which was to cement Pilate's place in the annals of history. To condemn Jesus, the Jews set out yet again to overrule their ruler.

By now it was early morning, and to avoid ceremonial uncleanness the Jews did not enter Pilate's palace.

> John 18:28-31
> Then the Jewish leaders took Jesus from Caiaphas to the palace of the Roman governor. By now it was early morning, and to avoid ceremonial uncleanness they did not enter the palace, because they wanted to be able to eat the Passover. So Pilate came out to them and asked, "What charges are you bringing against this man?" "If he were not a criminal," they replied, "we would not have handed him over to you." Pilate said, "Take him yourselves and judge him by your own law." "But we have no right to execute anyone," they objected.

It was early morning when word came that a detachment of the Jews, led by the high priest, were at the door asking for an audience with Pilate. The Jews wouldn't enter his palace because it was Gentile territory, unholy ground. According to Jewish laws, entering there would have made them unclean for seven days. The Jewish detachment wouldn't have been able to celebrate the Passover. Jewish law, found in Leviticus in the Old Testament and the Mishnah, a written version of Jewish oral law, are the sources of all codes regarding defilement. Incredibly, the priests were not concerned in the least about defiling themselves by conducting a clandestine and illegal trial! Hence Pilate went outside to learn what they wanted.

As the deputation approached with Jesus, it must have been obvious to

Pilate who the prisoner was. Jesus' face was swollen and red from the Sanhedrin's attacks. Scabs were forming where His beard had been torn out. His tunic was soiled and stained. His hair was in disarray. Despite His appearance, there was an aura about Jesus that Pilate found intriguing. Jesus carried Himself with dignity and stood silently in front of His accusers. Pilate's curiosity must have been roused watching Jesus and His captors.

When Pilate appeared, the crowd settled. The governor asked the leaders of the group, "What accusation do you bring against this man?" (John 18:29). The Jews were annoyed by this question. They'd told Pilate about Jesus when they'd requested a deputation of soldiers to arrest Him the previous night. They didn't want Pilate to know the real reason and couldn't announce that the capital charge upon the convicted was blasphemy for claiming He was God. After all, what harm could come from a person claiming to be God? Instead the Jewish leaders answered, "If He were not a criminal…we would not have handed him over to you" (John 18:30).

It's likely that Pilate didn't appreciate the Jewish leaders' haste. The Jews were in no position to demand approval of their conviction without another trial. Pilate may not have cared that a religious festival was occurring the next day. Given their history of misconduct, the governor was not required, or eager, to humor the Jewish leaders. Either they would treat him and his court with appropriate respect, and he would retry the case properly, or he wouldn't cooperate. "Take Him yourselves and judge Him" (John 18:31), Pilate declared, pretending to leave.

Luke 23:2

And they began to accuse him, saying, "We have found this man subverting our nation. He opposes payment of taxes to Caesar and claims to be Messiah, a king."

In an attempt to persuade Pilate to act, the Jewish leaders lied to him. They said, "We have found this man subverting our nation. He opposes payment of taxes to Caesar," despite the fact that Jesus had recently taught that it was lawful to pay taxes to Caesar (Luke 20:20-25). The Jewish leaders concluded: He "claims to be Christ, a king" (Luke 23:2). In truth, they understood the teachings of Jesus enough to realize that He was not calling Himself a king in a way that would concern Pilate or the Romans. Jesus had already told them about His kingdom in Heaven (Luke 22:67-69). Moreover, when the people had tried to make Him a political king earlier in His ministry, Jesus withdrew from them (John 6:15). He wasn't interested in pursuing an earthly rule. Nevertheless, the chief priests declared Jesus a kingdom-seeker on earth, which Pilate viewed as a possible threat to the Roman Empire. The Jewish leaders were desperate to win Pilate's judgment so they misrepresented Jesus' teachings.

If Jesus were a possible threat to the throne, Rome would require that Pilate investigate the matter to determine whether there was substance to the charge. But Pilate didn't want to question the accused in front of His enemies. He called for Jesus to enter the palace to discuss the matter privately.

John 18:33-38

Pilate then went back inside the palace, summoned Jesus and asked him, "Are you the king of the Jews?" "Is that your own idea," Jesus asked, "or did others talk to you about me?" "Am I a Jew?" Pilate replied. "Your own people and chief priests handed you over to me. What is it you have done?" Jesus said, "My kingdom is not of this world. If it were, my servants would fight to prevent my arrest by the Jewish leaders. But now my kingdom is from another place." "You are a king, then!" said Pilate. Jesus answered, "You say that I am a king. In fact, the reason I was born and came into the world is to testify to the truth. Everyone on the side of truth listens to me." "What is truth?" retorted Pilate. With this he went out again to the Jews gathered there and said, "I find no basis for a charge against him."

Pilate retreated into the privacy of his home and examined the prisoner. "Are you the king of the Jews?" he asked (John 18:33). Jesus answered with a question in return, which is often customary with Jewish people. "Is that your own idea," said Jesus, "or did others talk to you about me?" (John 18:33-34). Jesus was asking Pilate to examine his own motives in light of the circumstances. To Pilate's ears, though, Jesus' response must have sounded absurd. Jesus was the prisoner. Jesus was on trial. It's more than likely that Jesus' manner was becoming frustrating to Pilate. How and why was Jesus so calm and confident? Didn't He realize that He was on trial for His life? Pilate's rule was being challenged by a prisoner. Pilate's word was law, yet somehow, Jesus wasn't fearful of him.

"Am I a Jew?" Pilate replied. "It was your people and your chief priests who brought you to me. What is it you have done?" (John 18:35). Pilate's response implied two things. First, that he wanted to distance himself and the Gentiles from Jesus and the Jews by making it clear that he had no personal connection with them. At the same time, Pilate was emphasizing that Jesus' own people had put Him in that position and were calling for His death. What had He done to deserve such hatred and rejection?

Moved to respond, Jesus assured Pilate that His kingdom didn't belong to this world; it was no threat to Rome. If His kingdom were an earthly one Jesus argued, then His servants would be waging war in order to protect Him from Jewish persecution. Jesus repeated emphatically, "My kingdom is not of this world" (John 18:36). Hearing Jesus refer to His kingdom, Pilate asked his first question again. "Are you a king then?" (John 18:37).

Jesus affirmed that He was a king. He went on to explain the significance of His life and mission in this world: "For this reason I was born, and for this I came into the world, to testify to the truth. Everyone on the side of truth listens to me" (John 18:37). This was a remarkable statement for Jesus to make at that moment. He was accused of being a fraud by the Jewish leaders. His enemies were calling Him subversive and claiming that He was a liar and a deceiver. He was on trial for His life. Yet Jesus proclaimed Himself to be the source of truth.

Upon hearing Jesus' statement, Pilate's curiosity grew. It seemed impossible that Jesus wielded power over anyone, particularly in His vulnerable state. Jesus appeared deluded and harmless; not someone of significance and not worthy of death. Pilate left Jesus then and returned to the Jewish leaders. "What is truth?" (John 18:38) Pilate muttered to himself as he prepared to announce his verdict.

Luke 23:4-7
Then Pilate announced to the chief priests and the crowd, "I find no basis for a charge against this man." But they insisted, "He

stirs up the people all over Judea by his teaching. He started in Galilee and has come all the way here." On hearing this, Pilate asked if the man was a Galilean. When he learned that Jesus was under Herod's jurisdiction, he sent him to Herod, who was also in Jerusalem at that time.

"He is not guilty of any crime," declared Pilate to the expectant crowd. The chief priests were vehement and cried out with many accusations against Him. Four more times Pilate announced to the Jews that Jesus was not guilty (Luke 23:15; John 19:4; John 19:6; Matthew 27:24). At this point, Pilate was legally obligated to free Jesus and dismiss the crowd. To his detriment and Jesus', he allowed the crowd to continue to accuse Jesus.

We may never know why Pilate failed to dismiss the charges against Jesus and offer Him the protection of Rome. Perhaps he feared the crowd would riot if he dismissed the matter so easily. Whatever the reason, Pilate turned again and asked Jesus what He had done to deserve such infamy. "Are you not going to answer? See how many things they are accusing you of," (Mark 15:4). Jesus remained silent. He knew the law and it didn't require Him to answer the hateful charges the mob was hurling at Him. Pilate had declared His innocence. It was his responsibility to defend the ruling.

The demands of the Jewish leaders grew more urgent. They insisted that Jesus had been causing trouble since His teachings began in Galilee. Southern Jews considered Galileans lowlier believers; insufficiently faithful to the holy celebrations in Jerusalem and too inclined to adopt the secular habits and manner of dress of the Gentiles with whom they mixed. Common lore had it that insurrectionists came from Galilee so the plotters hoped that mentioning it would make Jesus seem more dangerous. Instead, Pilate seized upon the opportunity to extricate himself from the argument. He asked whether Jesus was a Galilean.

Discovering that He was, Pilate ruled that Herod Antipas, the Roman Governor of Galilee should preside over Jesus' trial and excused himself. Doing so released him from the conflict while allowing him to gain favour with Herod by showing him respect. Pilate's soldiers had killed a group of Galileans earlier so this was a way to repair the relationship with his counterpart. Since Herod happened to be in Jerusalem at the time, it was straightforward for Jesus to appear before him for further judgment.

Personal Reflections:

1. Pilate continuously provoked the Jewish leaders throughout his inglorious career as Governor of Judea. In turn, the Jews didn't hesitate to aggravate Pilate. Is there anyone in your life who seems to enjoy provoking you? How do you respond? Considering Jesus' way of reacting to Pilate and the Jewish leaders, how would you change your approach to people who provoke you?

2. Pilate knew that, legally, the correct course of action was to liberate Jesus from His captors, protect Him if necessary, and dismiss the crowd. Instead, Pilate disregarded the proper action, allowing the conflict to escalate and the crowd to grow more unruly. Have you ever been certain of the right thing to do but put off making the decision? What caused you to wait? Do you regret procrastinating?

3. The Jewish leaders knew that Jesus claimed to be a king in Heaven, but they altered the truth to manipulate Pilate. They believed that referring to a new kingdom would force Pilate to condemn Jesus with the ultimate punishment. Have you ever twisted the truth of a situation to mislead someone? Did you lie to protect someone close to you or for personal gain? How do you feel about your decision looking back?

Chapter 7

JESUS BEFORE HEROD

Luke 23:7
When he learned that Jesus was under Herod's jurisdiction, he sent him to Herod, who was also in Jerusalem at that time.

Herod Antipas was the governor of Galilee. He had similar political power to that of Pilate in Judea. However, there is no evidence of an acrimonious relationship between Herod and his Jewish subjects in Galilee. His weakness as a leader was the result of transgressions in his personal life. That weakness undermined his political prowess and ability to govern.

During a visit in Rome to see his half-brother Herod Philip, he encountered Philip's wife, Herodias. A highly ambitious and beautiful woman, she was bored with the life of a wealthy matron. She was tempted to have adventures with her brother-in-law in what was regarded as frontier country that eluded her life as a public personality with a banal husband in the safety of Rome. Herodias made a deal with Herod Antipas, promising her hand in marriage if he swore to divorce his current wife, the daughter of Aretas, the King of Petra. Herod agreed, and they were married soon after the arrangement. Herod Antipas and his new wife returned to Galilee, accompanied by Herodias' beautiful daughter, Salome.

This divorce and remarriage ensnared Herod Antipas in a scandal that greatly disturbed his Jewish subjects in Galilee. John the Baptist boldly and publicly denounced the union (Mark 6:18), proclaiming that such deeds were unlawful according to Jewish law (Leviticus 18:16). Not surprisingly, the Jewish leaders eagerly supported the denunciation of the governing couple. John the Baptist's public admonition severely embarrassed the couple and damaged the governor's reputation, which enraged Herodias. She wouldn't tolerate such humiliation and insisted that her husband arrest John the Baptist and send him to prison (Mark 6:17-20).

Prior to this incident, Herod Antipas had held John the Baptist in high favor. Even after imprisoning him, Herod often summoned John from his cell and listened to him preach. Herod Antipas and Herodias argued over John the Baptist's fate. Herodias was not pleased that he remained alive and argued for a more severe fate. However, we are told "Herod feared John and protected him, knowing him to be a righteous and holy man. When Herod heard John, he was greatly puzzled; yet he liked to listen to him" (Mark 6:20). Herodias, on the other hand, wanted John the Baptist executed.

Later, during Herod's birthday celebration, Herodias' beautiful daughter, Salome, danced before him and his guests. Drunk from too much wine and the young woman's intoxicating beauty, Herod promised her anything, even a gift that was on a par with half his kingdom. She went out to seek her mother's advice. After being persuaded by Herodias, Salome returned to Herod and asked him to give her John the Baptist's head on a platter. As the guests heard the young woman's request, Herod had no choice but to honor his word. The Gospel of Mark tells us that Herod was greatly upset by his wife's treacherous actions; but, he was bound by his word, so John the Baptist was beheaded (Mark 6:21-28).

Luke 23:8-9

When Herod saw Jesus, he was greatly pleased, because for a long time he had been wanting to see him. From what he had heard about him, he hoped to see him perform a sign of some sort. He plied him with many questions, but Jesus gave him no answer.

Soon after John the Baptist's beheading, Herod became acquainted with Jesus' teachings and growing fame. The governor may have feared that Jesus was John the Baptist raised from the dead. If so, Herod might be condemned again for his sinful relationship with his brother's wife. But Jesus didn't condemn him and Herod's fear gradually became admiration for Jesus' remarkable miracles. Herod had heard amazing things about Jesus' powers, which were said to include healing the sick, causing the blind to see, and raising people from the dead. Such powers had never been heard of before. Herod avidly desired an audience with Jesus if only to witness Him performing some miracles.

When Jesus was presented to Herod for a final trial settlement He wasn't at risk of immediate condemnation. On the contrary, Herod was genuinely excited to meet Him. The Jews under Herod's jurisdiction didn't provide him with much entertainment. He might have thought an audience with Jesus and the opportunity to watch miracles performed would be amusing.

Herod was so enthusiastic about having Jesus presented to him by Pilate, that he disregarded the purpose for His appearance. Herod wasn't interested in the Jews' "trifling squabbles" either — particularly in matters that didn't concern the Gentiles. The Galileans had long been accused of being revolutionists and Herod was most likely bored by this kind of gossip. He didn't believe that Jesus was a traitor or a threat to Rome, and the prisoner didn't appear to be dangerous as the Jewish leaders claimed.

It says in Luke 23:9 that Herod "plied [Jesus] with many questions." Herod welcomed Jesus and began to question Him about His amazing power. Some of the questions might have included the following. What were the greatest of His miracles? Could He perform them in front of the court? How long had He had these abilities? Did He confer the same powers on His followers?

During this onslaught of questions, Jesus didn't speak a word. He simply stood in silence, calmly observing the man who'd murdered His cousin, John the Baptist. Finally, Herod realized that his guest was not offering any form of response or explanation for His deeds. Was this man afraid of him? What was the matter?

Then it might have dawned on Herod that Jesus was unwilling to engage him in conversation. He was also unwilling to entertain the court with miracles. Herod's amusement quickly turned to anger and frustration. Who did this man think He was? Had Herod not been polite and deferred to Him? Why did He refuse to please the court? Herod had eagerly welcomed Jesus, but now Herod was offended.

Herod failed to recognize that Jesus wasn't an entertainer. Miracles weren't meant to amuse and beguile the public. His miracles were sparingly performed for the immediate benefit of His subject. Miracles were also performed to bring attention to His identity, calling people to listen to

His teachings. In the Gospel of John, miracles were called "signs." In other words, each sign represented a reality and a meaning beyond the miracle itself. For example, in John 6:1-13, with one boy's meal consisting of five, small, barley loaves and two little fish, Jesus fed five thousand men. He didn't merely want to give the people a meal; He wanted them to know His power as Creator. The next morning, as recorded in John 6:26, Jesus criticized the crowd for only coming to Him because He had filled their stomachs and not because they'd recognized the sign of creation. The night of the betrayal, He said to His followers, "Believe me when I say that I am in the Father and the Father is in me; or at least believe the evidence of the miracles themselves" (John 14:11). Like the thousands whom Jesus fed, Herod was uninterested in the identity of Jesus. His only desire was to be amazed.

Jesus wouldn't perform miracles before Herod. Heavenly power was never to be used for His convenience. Herod, in contrast, delighted in amusing himself and his guests by any available means. Jesus refused to satisfy people's curiosity. He revealed Himself only to those who truly and earnestly pursued Him and His message. He always spoke to those who were determined to reach the Father. To a man like Herod, Jesus had nothing to say.

Luke 23: 10-12

The chief priests and the teachers of the law were standing there, vehemently accusing him. Then Herod and his soldiers ridiculed and mocked him. Dressing him in an elegant robe, they sent him back to Pilate. That day Herod and Pilate became friends—before this they had been enemies.

If Jesus wouldn't entertain the court with a display of miracles, Herod was determined to find other forms of entertainment. He and his soldiers began mocking Jesus, ridiculing the powerful man who wouldn't use His power or even His words to defend Himself. Although He saved others, He wouldn't save Himself! The soldiers vied to mock Jesus. Their efforts came to fruition when a cast-off but gorgeous robe was brought to Herod. The soldiers clothed Jesus in it and pretended to pay homage to Him. With this showcase of ridicule in progress, Herod must have nearly forgotten that he hadn't been shown any miracles.

After Herod and his soldiers had grown tired of their sport, he considered the crimes that had been credited to Jesus. He couldn't find the man guilty, in spite of all the accusations hurled upon Him by the chief priests. So, Herod deferred the matter back to Pilate sending the message that he didn't find Jesus to be worthy of death. In fact, Herod reportedly didn't find Jesus guilty of any crime (Luke 23:15). The question of Jesus' guilt had only been prolonged by His appearance before Herod. Despite the lack of resolution, Pilate and Herod made peace with each other that day and became good friends.

Personal Reflections:

1. Herod was a person before whom Jesus remained silent. We can imagine why Jesus didn't address this man: Herod had murdered His beloved cousin, and he didn't desire an intimate understanding of God's Word. What would you say to Herod to change his mind? Given Jesus' position, is silence the better option at such a time? When have you felt the urge to speak to your enemy but remained silent?

2. Jesus was mocked by the soldiers, one of the most frustrating indignities that anyone could endure. Think about a time when you or someone you know has been bullied or mocked. What thoughts went through your mind? How did you want to respond? How did you actually respond? What is the proper response, according to Jesus' example?

3. Jesus could have easily performed some miracle so as to appease Herod in the court. It would have been easy for Jesus to entertain him in order to regain His freedom, yet Jesus refused to compromise Himself or His relationship with God in that way. Simply put, Jesus didn't take the easy way out. Have you been tempted to take the easy way out in a situation by making an immoral or wrong decision? How can we strengthen ourselves so that we take the right path through the difficult situations in our lives? How can you personally avoid taking "shortcuts" in making challenging decisions?

4. It's unfortunate that many people attend church for the entertainment they receive from the service. Those people have a "Herod mentality." Jesus

doesn't cater to peoples' amusement or their ulterior motives as we see by His appearance before Herod. Why do people prefer a show or something eye-catching instead of what Jesus offers? Does our society influence this mindset? How? What do you look for in a church service or a religious group?

Chapter 8

JESUS RETURNS TO PILATE

Luke 23: 13-16; 18-25,
Pilate called together the chief priests, the rulers and the people, and
said to them, "You brought me this man as one who was inciting the
people to rebellion. I have examined him in your presence and have
found no basis for your charges against him. Neither has Herod,
for he sent him back to us; as you can see, he has done nothing to
deserve death. Therefore, I will punish him and then release him. "

But the whole crowd shouted, "Away with this man! Release Barabbas
to us!" (Barabbas had been thrown into prison for an insurrection in
the city, and for murder.) Wanting to release Jesus, Pilate appealed
to them again. But they kept shouting, "Crucify him! Crucify him!"
For the third time he spoke to them: "Why? What crime has this man
committed? I have found in him no grounds for the death penalty.
Therefore I will have him punished and then release him." But with
loud shouts they insistently demanded that he be crucified, and
their shouts prevailed. So Pilate decided to grant their demand. He
released the man who had been thrown into prison for insurrection
and murder, the one they asked for, and surrendered Jesus to their
will.

When Jesus returned before Pilate, it became clear to him that Jesus was
not a criminal and therefore must be released. Pilate summoned the chief
priests and rulers to provide his assessment of the trial. The governor
explained that Jesus had been brought to him as one who incites the people
to rebellion, but he had found nothing to validate the charge. Further,
Herod's examination of the case had supported Pilate's position on the
matter. There simply was no evidence against Jesus.

Matthew 27:19
While Pilate was sitting on the judge's seat, his wife sent him this

message: "Don't have anything to do with that innocent man, for I
have suffered a great deal today in a dream because of him."

The disturbance of the arresting mob outside her window awoke Pilate's
wife Claudia. Inquiring about the commotion she learned—to her
horror—that her husband was involved in a trial of the man who had
appeared in her nightmare. Claudia had heard rumors about Jesus, and her
husband had possibly mentioned the Jewish petition for soldiers the night
before. She was certain that her husband should have no dealings with
Jesus. With great haste, she sent a message to her husband warning him
not to get involved with Jesus' trial and referred to Him as an "innocent
man" (Matthew 27:19). This confirmation of Jesus' innocence spoke loudly
to Pilate. He too was very troubled about Jesus, and to him, this was no
dream!

John 19:1
Then Pilate took Jesus and had Him flogged.

Then Pilate gave the order for Jesus to suffer a Roman scourging. There was
a monumental difference between a flogging at the hand of the Jews and
one by the Romans. With a Jewish flogging, the victim could not receive
more than forty lashes, according to the Law of Moses (Deuteronomy
25:1-3); however, the Romans were not familiar with the Law of Moses.
They flogged the victim until they were satisfied. The instrument used for
flogging had a short, rigid handle to which several leather thongs were
attached. To the loose end of each thong, a sharp piece of bone or metal
was fastened. When the pieces of leather hit the person, they would inflict
sufficient injury to raise ugly welts. The sharp instruments on the end of
the thongs would cut and tear off pieces of skin, muscle tissue, or scalp.
Often an eye would be lost, and the person could suffer mutilations as a
result of the beating. Many of the victims were so harshly wounded that
they died before being cut down from the Roman whipping post.

Jesus was lashed to the whipping post with His chest and stomach against
it. His arms were wrapped around the post—as if hugging it—and securely
tied. He was stripped, His back and legs exposed to the soldier wielding
the whip. Then the strokes began.

69

Usually those being flogged would scream and beg for mercy. There is no record in the of how Jesus reacted to being flogged, yet there are prophecies in the Old Testament that predicted the suffering that Jesus would experience and how He would bear that suffering. Isaiah 53:7 tells us that Jesus would bear the punishment in silence: "He was oppressed and afflicted, yet He did not open his mouth." Isaiah prophesied what Jesus would look like as a result of the punishment: "Just as there were many who were appalled at Him. His appearance was so disfigured beyond that of any man, and His form marred beyond human likeness" (Isaiah 52:14). So viciously had the soldiers scourged Jesus that once they'd finished, Jesus ceased to look human. He was bruised and bleeding from innumerable marks on His body. Here we have one more illegal act perpetrated against Jesus. Such was the rough justice of the Romans.

Aside: There appears to be a contradiction in the ordering of events in the gospels among John, Matthew, and Mark. In Matthew and Mark, Jesus' flogging seems to occur after the sentence of crucifixion. The sentence of crucifixion itself is not recorded in these gospels; it is stated that Pilate delivered Jesus to be crucified when he had had Him scourged. The Gospel of John, however, places the scourging well before the sentencing. It is thought that John has the order of events properly recorded and that Matthew and Mark simply document what events transpire and in no particular order. This writing is not to be considered a fault necessarily. At times, gospels do not concern themselves with the chronological order of events in their documentation. Instead, the gospels include the events without noting their timely occurrence in relation to other events.

Matthew 27: 27-30
Then the governor's soldiers took Jesus into the Praetorium
and gathered the whole company of soldiers around him. They
stripped him and put a scarlet robe on him, and then twisted
together a crown of thorns and set it on his head. They put a staff
in his right hand. Then they knelt in front of him and mocked
him. "Hail, king of the Jews!" they said. They spit on him, and
took the staff and struck him on the head again and again.

The soldiers were not done with Jesus yet. They found a purple robe and draped it over His bleeding shoulders. Then one of them stepped outside

70

to collect some thorny brambles and wove a crown to press down over His brow. After all, did not this man claim to be a king in their very presence? Then each one approached Him in turn and greeted Him as a king, striking Him on the face and spitting upon Him. It was probably great fun for them, and so they enjoyed the chance to humiliate Him. Jesus stood silently as they carried on their vulgar game.

John 19:4-5

Once more Pilate came out and said to the Jews gathered there, "Look, I am bringing him out to you to let you know that I find no basis for a charge against him." When Jesus came out wearing the crown of thorns and the purple robe, Pilate said to them, "Here is the man!"

Soon Pilate called for Jesus to return. The crowd was becoming even more restless, and the governor wanted to close the matter. Going out himself to face the people, Pilate declared for the third time the innocence of Jesus (John 19:4). Then he motioned for the soldiers to bring Jesus to them. Jesus stumbled out wearing the purple robe and the crown of thorns. The crowd likely gasped in amazement at the sight of Him, He'd been so badly beaten by the Romans. The high priests would have had trouble recognizing Him as the once-composed subject of their hatred.

Pilate then spoke memorable words: "Here is the man!" (John 19:5). This statement is ironic because it describes exactly what every preacher of the Gospel urges people to do, that is, to consider Christ. It was a remarkable moment, for that is exactly what the people did—but they did not see Jesus as a Savior, nor even as one to be pitied as Pilate had wanted them to.

What Pilate probably sought from the crowd was pity. He may have believed that any reasonable person would gaze upon Jesus with a sense of sorrow, perhaps even shame for what had been done to Him. After all, the soldiers had humiliated Him to the very limits of the human imagination. They had tortured him nearly to the point of death. What more could the Jewish leaders want? Had the troublemaker not been shamed, punished and dishonored enough? Should the people not relent and release Him?

Matthew 27:6-7

The chief priests picked up the coins and said, "It is against the law to put this into the treasury, since it is blood money." So they decided to use the money to buy the potter's field as a burial place for foreigners.

"Crucify Him! Crucify Him," came the blood-thirsty Jewish leaders' response. Pilate scarcely believed his ears, witnessing such aggression toward someone who appeared so harmless and helpless. Clearly, Pilate's subjects were remarkably determined. They wouldn't be deterred from their persecution of Jesus.

For the fourth time, Pilate declared, "You take Him and crucify Him. As for me, I find no basis for a charge against Him." (John 19:6). While his command was clear, Pilate failed to mandate the immediate release of the prisoner, which belied his judgment, as well as his fourth acquittal of Jesus. In lieu of disbanding the crowd, Pilate's inaction fueled the hope of the leaders that they would yet prevail in the trial. In truth, a flogging was a common precursor to crucifixion in the Roman system.

Aside: It is a fact that the Jews had four forms of capital punishment: stoning, strangling, beheading, and burning. Stoning was the common form of punishment at the time; it is, therefore, interesting that in Jesus' case the Jews cried "crucify" and desired that Jesus be put to death by a Roman form of execution. Crucifixion was a very slow way to die. The victim would suffer for hours or even days, whereas the various forms of Jewish execution only lasted for seconds or minutes, so the victim wouldn't suffer long. This explanation tells us that the Jews wanted to make Jesus suffer as much as possible; Crucifixion would also provide them with further opportunities to humiliate Him as He hung on the cross.

Matthew 27:17

So when the crowd had gathered, Pilate asked them, "Which one do you want me to release to you: Jesus Barabbas, or Jesus who is called the Messiah?

Nothing is known in history of Barabbas, though Matthew 27:16 calls him "notorious," and the language in Mark 15:7 suggests that Barabbas' criminal activity of insurrection and murder was notorious in his generation.

John 19:7-11

The Jewish leaders insisted, "We have a law, and according to that law he must die, because he claimed to be the Son of God." When Pilate heard this, he was even more afraid, and he went back inside the palace. "Where do you come from?" he asked Jesus, but Jesus gave him no answer. "Do you refuse to speak to me?" Pilate said. "Don't you realize I have power either to free you or to crucify you?" Jesus answered, "You would have no power over me if it were not given to you from above. Therefore the one who handed me over to you is guilty of a greater sin.

Realizing that the charges they had leveled against Jesus so far would not sway Pilate's opinion on the case, the Jewish leaders finally confessed the real reason they wanted Jesus dead: He had committed blasphemy. He had called Himself God. Now that the truth was spoken, it had a remarkable effect on Pilate. In John 19:8, the writer tells us that when Pilate learned of Jesus' claim to deity, he was even more afraid. Fear had been creeping into Pilate's heart concerning this man, and now his fear had reached its peak.

Leaving the crowd seething outside, Pilate entered the palace to have a private audience with Jesus. "Where do you come from?" (John 19:9), he inquired. Pilate knew that Jesus was from Galilee, that much had been made clear. Therefore, Pilate wasn't asking Jesus from where in this world He came but from what world He came.

There was a superstition among the Romans at that time that some of their gods visited the world disguised as men. People needed to be very careful about how they treated these gods for fear of reprisal from the underworld. This might have been what Pilate was thinking and what fueled his fear. He'd been extremely cruel and unjust to Jesus. What if Jesus were a god?

Pilate's question to Jesus just hung in the silence there of the palace. Once more, Jesus confounded His enemies with His silence. Pilate might have noticed the difference between Jesus' quiet, peaceful demeanor and his own agitation. Why would the man not speak? Why didn't he recognize authority? Pilate asked Jesus, "Do you refuse to speak to me? Do not you realize I have power to free you or to crucify you?" (John 19:10). Pilate's reaction to Jesus' silence stood in stark contrast to that of Herod. Pilate seemed uneasy with the situation he was in; he feared the people would riot and he wanted to be rid of Jesus.

Jesus had been silent before the Sanhedrin and Herod, but He looked calmly at Pilate through swollen eyes and answered him: "You would have no power over me if it were not given to you from above. Therefore, the one who handed me over to you is guilty of a greater sin." Within this response, Jesus delivered two startling and loaded messages. First, Jesus reminded Pilate that his authority over Him was not his own; it had been given to him by someone greater—a higher power. Jesus was pointing out that Pilate wasn't the ultimate authority although he would be accountable for the actions he took using his derived power. It was a gentle but effective way for Jesus to rebuke Pilate and warn him to be cautious in his actions. It didn't make any difference whether Pilate believed that the higher authority was Caesar or God.

Jesus' second message also sought to unnerve Pilate by warning him about the dangerous path he'd chosen. Jesus said that the one who'd delivered Him to Pilate was guilty of the "greater" sin. Jesus may have been referring to Judas here. Judas had positioned himself as Jesus' friend, known about His teachings and power and yet betrayed Him. This would account for his greater sin. Regardless of whom Jesus was referencing, He was implying that Pilate was also guilty of grievous sins. Pilate continually maintained that Jesus was not guilty but hadn't released Him. After Jesus' quiet accusation, Pilate must have felt even more determined to disband the prosecution.

John 19:12-16
From then on, Pilate tried to set Jesus free, but the Jewish leaders kept shouting, "If you let this man go, you are no friend of Caesar. Anyone who claims to be a king opposes Caesar." When Pilate heard this, he brought Jesus out and sat down on the judge's seat at a place known as the Stone Pavement (which in Aramaic is Gabbatha). It was the day of Preparation of the Passover; it was about noon. "Here is your king," Pilate said to the Jews. But they shouted, "Take him away! Take him away! Crucify him!" "Shall

I crucify your king?" Pilate asked. "We have no king but Caesar," the chief priests answered. Finally Pilate handed him over to them to be crucified.

Returning once again to the Jews, Pilate argued for Jesus' life, although his efforts would ultimately make no difference. The power dynamic between the Jewish leaders and him was changing. Earlier on, the Jews had pled for Jesus to be executed and Pilate had wielded his authority over them, refusing to be manipulated. Now, the Jews were demanding Jesus' life. Pilate was fearful of losing control of the situation.

The Jewish leaders had hit upon a powerful and persuasive approach to manipulate him. "If you let this man go, you are no friend of Caesar. Anyone who claims to be a king opposes Caesar" (John 19:12). Pilate would certainly fear offending Caesar, who was the ultimate human authority and extremely volatile. Pilate may have believed that if he released Jesus, the Jews would file another petition complaining about him to the emperor. Moreover, this petition had the potential to capture Caesar's attention beyond other appeals since the Jews would claim that a serious opponent of the Roman Empire had been released. Pilate wouldn't risk an investigation by Caesar.

Everyone knew that the Caesar of that time, Tiberias, was little more than a madman. He conducted a reign of terror among his underlings so as to maintain the utmost power. Furthermore, his suspicions were easily aroused by the slightest rumors of treason. The threat of going before Caesar broke the spine of Pilate's resolve and caused him to surrender to the constant barrage from his Jewish subjects. The Jews had turned from attacking Jesus to attacking Pilate, it was a successful tactic. Their victory was at hand.

Even as he inwardly resigned himself to losing the battle of releasing Jesus, Pilate saw an opportunity to make sport of the Jews. In truth, the Jews had implied a profession of loyalty to Caesar by threatening to appear before him. So, Pilate pointed to Jesus and said, "Behold your king!" The Jews were enraged and cried again for Him to be crucified. "Shall I crucify your king?" taunted Pilate. "We have no king but Caesar" (John 19:15), they screamed. Pilate must have taken great satisfaction from hearing the

Jewish leaders pledge allegiance to Caesar.

Matthew 27:24-25

When Pilate saw that he was getting nowhere, but that instead an uproar was starting, he took water and washed his hands in front of the crowd. "I am innocent of this man's blood," he said. "It is your responsibility!" All the people answered, "His blood is on us and on our children!"

Pilate's minor triumph was not to be compared to the violation of justice that he was about to commit. Calling for a basin and towel, he theatrically washed his hands of the matter before the people and confessed the innocence of Jesus for a fifth and final time. The crowd tasted victory as it witnessed the hand washing and heard Pilate's words. The people assumed full responsibility for the Galilean's death as they shouted back to Pilate, "Let His blood be on us and on our children" (Matthew 27:25). Then their anger against Pilate dissolved into the joy of conquest. Jesus would be put to death, but not before He was subjected to a final mockery.

Aside: Following the persecution of Jesus, Pilate, interestingly enough, clung to office for another six years. In the spring of 37 A.D., he blundered over an apparent insurrection in Samaria. While trying to quell an angry, armed mob, his troops slaughtered a great number of the crowd. An appeal immediately went out to Vitellius and he, upon investigating the charges, suspended Pilate from office and sent him back to Rome. While Pilate was en route there, Tiberius the emperor died and the case supposedly got lost in bureaucracy. An unproven reference to Pilate committing suicide in 39 A.D. appears in the writings of Eusebius. In the end, Pilate is most remembered as the man who tried Jesus, proclaimed Him not guilty, and then, condemned Him to death.

Matthew 27:31

After they had mocked him, they took off the robe and put his own clothes on him. Then they led him away to crucify him.

The Gentiles took their turn at mocking Jesus as recorded in Mark 15:16-19 and Matthew 27:27-30. The entire band of soldiers joined in. The indignities perpetrated against Him included dressing Him as a king in a purple robe with a crown of thorns, and a mock scepter made from a reed. Again, Jesus was subjected to blows to the face, spitting, and feigned homage. The Gentiles rivaled the Jews in their abuse of the innocent man.

The soldiers had their orders to execute the sentence. They put Jesus back in His own clothes, gathered up rope, nails and a hammer and arranged for the crosses to be transported. Then they brought Jesus to the place of crucifixion.

Personal Reflections:

1. During the trials before the Jewish leaders, and then Pilate and Herod, Jesus was the target of false accusations. He said and did very little to defend Himself. In fact, He used silence effectively to maintain His control of the situation. The few words He spoke were designed to expose His captors' sinful motives. Consider a situation in which you were wrongfully accused of something. Would you ever be willing to wait for the Lord to vindicate your reputation in His own time?

2. Finding no concrete evidence against Jesus, Pilate had full legal authority to release Him. Instead, he allowed the people's will to prevail, despite knowing that they were acting unjustly. Have you ever been in a situation where someone was being falsely accused but you didn't speak in their defense? Why did you remain silent? Was it to protect your reputation or standing with the crowd? Were you afraid of the crowd's reaction to you? What would you do differently if you could revisit the situation?

3. Pilate washed his hands of Jesus — to avoid being involved with the bogus trial and judgment. Even so, he couldn't escape God's judgment. What excuses have you made to absolve yourself of guilt? Will they stand up to God's judgment? What should we strive to do instead when these difficult situations arise?

Chapter 9

VIA DOLOROSA

Luke 23: 26

At 6:30 in the morning, the early-rising Jewish people were awake and well into their day. Already, word had spread that the popular teacher Jesus, had been arrested, tried, and condemned to death. The people could scarcely believe their ears. Only a few days earlier, Jesus had been the center of a triumphant march into Jerusalem (Mark 11:1-11; Matthew 21:1-17; Luke 19:19-44). He had routed the religious leaders in public debate. The crowds had loved Him. Now, He was being led away to be crucified. How could things have gone so terribly wrong?

In all likelihood, the Galilean Jews who welcomed Jesus and clung to Him during His triumphant entry into Jerusalem (Matthew 21:11) were there for the Passover celebrations. The holiday mood would explain their enthusiasm toward Him. By contrast, their calmer, southern cousins, Judean Jews, who lived in the city, hadn't shown as much interest in Jesus during His ministry. This might explain how the Jewish leadership was able to whip up support for Jesus' crucifixion just a few days after His rousing reception. Nevertheless, the pace of change was astounding. People thronged the streets asking each other questions, then headed to Pilate's quarters, the last place that Jesus was reported to have been taken.

Roman law mandated a ten-day delay between sentencing and carrying out the death penalty. The convicted felon was given time to put his affairs in order. No such consideration was shown Jesus that morning, perhaps because He wasn't a Roman citizen. Instead, He was rushed from the place of sentencing to the place of execution with remarkable haste.

The road He traveled from the Roman Praetorium to the place of crucifixion was called Via Dolorosa, "the way of suffering." H. V. Morton suggests that it was "mercifully short – scarcely a thousand paces." Often called a death march, the walk served as an opportunity for the public to view the guilty ones, and a warning to those considering a life of crime. The crowd usually taunted the condemned en route to the place of execution, adding torment to the person's already miserable experience. Such sport was often engaged in with great enthusiasm.

Death occurred outside the walled city as a show of society's total rejection of the criminal. This practice also prevented the Passover from being tainted by a terrible event.

The purpose of having the condemned carry his own cross was twofold: it weakened him—ensuring less resistance at the death site—and the act enlisted his help in his own execution. In John 19:17, we are told that Jesus began the death march carrying His own cross. However, Matthew, Mark, and Luke all record that Simon of Cyrene, a pilgrim on his way into Jerusalem, was soon forced to carry the cross for Him. This was likely Simon's first encounter with Jesus, although it was not necessarily the last. We are once again confronted with Jesus' remarkable power to draw people to Himself, regardless of what the world thought of Him.

Aside: Mark mentions that this Simon had a son named Rufus, who was known to the readers of his gospel. Simon and his sons may have become followers of Jesus. If the Rufus mentioned in Mark 15:21 is the same man that Paul mentions in Romans 16:13, then it was Simon's wife who became a mother-figure to Paul. We can only speculate on what transpired during this providential encounter between Simon and Jesus.

Luke 23: 27-32

A large number of people followed him, including women who mourned and wailed for him. Jesus turned and said to them, "Daughters of Jerusalem, do not weep for me; weep for yourselves and for your children. For the time will come when you will say, 'Blessed are the childless women, the wombs that never bore and the breasts that never nursed!' Then " 'they will say to the mountains, "Fall on us!" and to the hills, "Cover us!" ' For if people do these things when the tree is green, what will happen when it is dry?" Two other men, both criminals, were also led out with him to be executed.

As the crowds parted in the street to allow the procession to pass, Jesus saw many women weeping at the sight of Him. Jesus spoke to them specifically, as they were expressing sorrow at what was being done to Him. As He spoke, Jesus' thoughts traveled to a future scene, the siege of Jerusalem and the weeping that would take place at that time.

Previously, Jesus had prophesied the destruction of Jerusalem, as recorded in Luke 21: 20-24: "When you see Jerusalem being surrounded by armies, you will know that its desolation is near. Then let those who are in Judea flee to the mountains, let those in the city get out, and let those in the country not enter the city. For this is the time of punishment in fulfillment of all that has been written. How dreadful it will be in those days for pregnant women and nursing mothers! There will be great distress in the land and wrath against this people. They will fall by the sword and will be taken as prisoners to all the nations." This fall of Jerusalem that Jesus referred to earlier in His ministry and on His way to the cross did indeed take place. In 66 AD, Jerusalem revolted against Roman rule. In 70 AD, Titus, a Roman general, besieged the city and eventually conquered it for Rome. The suffering and death toll, among Jewish fighters and civilians, was enormous.

On His way to the cross, Jesus spoke to the women about that future day, a disaster that would come in their lifetime and prove to be far worse than the present circumstance. Jesus called on the women to stop weeping for Him and weep for themselves and the great sorrow that would be theirs.

He compared Himself to a green tree that wasn't good for burning. He explained that even though He wasn't good for burning, He was suffering enormous persecution at the hands of the Jewish leaders. He then compared the women to dry trees that made good fuel for burning; therefore the persecution they would suffer at the hands of the Romans would be far greater. If crucifixion was the judgment on Him, who'd done nothing to deserve it, what would it be on those who were worthy of it? What would it be on the women, who lacked Jesus' innocence? It was a somber comparison that Jesus made with a heart full of compassion.

Personal Reflections:

1. In the gospels, only positive statements are made about women in relationship to Jesus. No woman was said to have betrayed Him or deserted Him. They made no empty boasts about remaining loyal, regardless of the cost. They weren't numbered among the false witnesses against Him. They didn't spit in His face or mock Him in any manner. Instead, one woman washed His feet with her tears (Luke 7:38), and anointed His feet with ointment (Luke 7:46). Tradition also tells us that women sent the wine laced with an analgesic to the place of execution so as to show mercy to the victims (Matthew 27:33-34). Women were the last at the tomb on Friday and the first present on the morning of the resurrection (Mark 15:40-41; Mark 16:1). Following the resurrection, the first two appearances of Christ were before women. They announced to the others that Jesus was alive (Matthew 28:5-8; John 20:11-18; Matthew 28:9-10). In fact, the gospels show the aggressive evil of the men, but not of the women. People who seek to use the Scriptures to limit women's role in society and the church gloss over the gospels and these facts. Women tend to be the more compassionate members of society in every age and are frequently the more spiritually enterprising. Women accompanied Jesus during His 3 ½ years of ministry and helped finance the mission (Luke 8:1-3). Jesus has honored women greatly and bestowed upon them a dignity that's been stolen from them by ecclesiastical authority over the ages. Why are we so slow to call upon women to minister among us and use their gifts for the common good?

2. En route to the cross, Jesus was consumed with His own suffering, yet He still ministered to the needs of the women of Jerusalem. We're told in the Scriptures that Jesus is the same, yesterday, today, and forever (Hebrews 13:8). Therefore, we believe that He's never too busy to pay attention to the needs of any one of us. We may confidently come to Him full of assurance that He'll listen carefully and give full attention to our personal needs and concerns. In light of this compassion and unconditional love, what causes you to hesitate to bring your needs to Jesus? What causes you to doubt His love for you or His willingness to listen?

3. When Jesus was on His way to the cross, He encountered Simon, which entirely changed the direction of Simon's life. Have you considered the

good that may come from your suffering? People watch how you cope with tragedy and may ask the source of or the reason for your endurance. This gives you the opportunity to tell them how God helped you, just as the Apostle Paul did throughout his physical trials (2 Corinthians 12:7-10). How does God provide you with a source of strength? Do you allow yourself to rely on His love? Why or why not?

Chapter 10

THE PLACE OF THE SKULL

Mark 15:22-23
They brought Jesus to the place called Golgotha (which means
"the place of the skull"). Then they offered him wine mixed with
myrrh, but he did not take it.

The term Golgotha is derived from Aramaic and means "The Place of
the Skull." In Latin, the term becomes "Calvary" in English. There's a
dispute over Golgotha's exact location. The traditional position places it
towards the western side of Jerusalem. Scripture tells us that the burial
site was outside the city wall. So the traditional site at the Church of the
Holy Sepulchre inside the wall seems wrong. The Gordon's Calvary site is
located more towards the center of Jerusalem and much farther north than
the traditional position. While there are arguments that the traditional site
might be outside the city wall, the Gordon's Calvary has the appearance of
a skull from a distance and thus seems the more probable site.

Upon reaching the execution site, the four soldiers in charge of the
prisoners decided the order in which the victims would be crucified. The
soldiers didn't hesitate to offer the drug-laced wine to the victims before
nailing them to crosses.

Aside: Myrrh is considered a narcotic: It was used for perfume and
embalming but it also dulled the senses and lessened pain when taken
internally. It made the soldiers' job easier if the prisoners didn't feel the full
sensation of pain while they were being secured to the crosses. There was
usually enough time between crucifixion and death for the wine to wear
off and the full physical suffering to be endured.

Jesus refused the wine once He'd tasted it. He recognized that it would
reduce His suffering by dulling the pain and clouding His mind. He didn't
want to lose control of His thoughts as He still had work to do while

enduring crucifixion for six hours before dying. Thus, Jesus chose to face His suffering conscious and aware of all that transpired. He didn't resist the soldiers' efforts to nail Him to the cross so they didn't force Him to take the wine.

John 19:18
There they crucified him, and with him two others—one on each side and Jesus in the middle.

Roman citizens were usually spared the indignity of crucifixion when executed. As an alternative, a more humane method, such as beheading, was employed. Romans were crucified only in extreme cases, such as high treason against the emperor. It is probable, then, that the criminals who were crucified with Jesus weren't Romans. People recognized the barbaric elements in this form of death. It was considered the most painful manner in which to die.

The one appointed to complete the crucifixion would step forward and strip the victim. The dignity of modesty was denied, the victim was totally exposed. Then the one in charge would command the victim to lie down on the cross. Crosses came in several shapes including the traditional "T," "X" or stake. Jesus was likely crucified on a "T"-shaped cross because a sign was placed above His head (Matt. 27:37). Usually the person was crucified head up, but some executioners demanded that the victim be crucified with his head down. Other soldiers would often be needed to prevent the victim from resisting as he was laid upon the cross. The victim's limbs were lashed to the cross with ropes to bear the body's weight. Then a hammer was used to drive spikes through the hands and feet, adding dramatically to the victim's suffering.

Once the person was securely attached to the cross, the soldiers organized themselves around guy ropes to lift the cross and lower it into a hole in the ground. The victim was usually a foot or two off the ground and able to partially stabilize himself by sitting on a small piece of wood jutting out of the upright beam. Based on medical experts' analyses, it is believed that the victim had to pull up with the hands or push up with the feet in order to take each breath. The victim had to exert himself just to breathe. The strain on the nail-pierced extremities greatly intensified the agony.

However, the victims' most common complaint was the dreadful thirst they felt as they baked under the hot Palestinian sun. Death came when the exhausted victim finally suffocated, unable to lift himself up anymore to breathe.

John 19:18-22
Pilate had a notice prepared and fastened to the cross. It read: JESUS OF NAZARETH, THE KING OF THE JEWS. Many of the Jews read this sign, for the place where Jesus was crucified was near the city, and the sign was written in Aramaic, Latin and Greek. The chief priests of the Jews protested to Pilate, "Do not write 'The King of the Jews,' but that this man claimed to be king of the Jews." Pilate answered, "What I have written, I have written."

Posting the notice above Jesus on the cross and leaving it unchanged, Pilate asserted himself against the Jewish leaders' wishes. Pilate wasn't insulting Jesus with this notice. He was signaling to the Jewish leaders that, as a Roman governor, he had the right to crucify the King of the Jews. Finally, Pilate had won a victory over the Jewish leaders; unfortunately, it was too late to serve the cause of justice.

John 19:24
Let's not tear it," they said to one another. "Let's decide by lot who will get it." This happened that the scripture might be fulfilled that said, "They divided my clothes among them and cast lots for my garment." So this is what the soldiers did.

Matthew 27:36
And sitting down, they kept watch over him there.

Once the victims were suspended on their crosses, their few personal effects could be divided by the soldiers. Then they were assigned to keep watch until death slowly overtook the condemned. In the case of extremely strong people, it could take several days for death to come, but for most people it took less time. Watching over the condemned was the uneventful aspect of the soldiers' task. It kept them away from their families and provided little entertainment in return.

Personal Reflections:

1. The common form of execution among the Jews was stoning. This punishment only lasted a few minutes. After a few blows to the head, the victim would be rendered unconscious and unaware of his suffering. Crucifixion, by contrast, was the most agonizing and shameful form of execution. By suffering on the cross for our sin, Jesus accepted the worst punishment possible at that time. He refused the wine laced with myrrh so as to feel the full pain of the crucifixion. His immense suffering happened in public and He endured everything out of love for us. Why do we still question His love? Why do we find it challenging sometimes to trust in Him?

Chapter 11

THE WORDS OF FORGIVENESS

Luke 23:34
Father, forgive them for they do not know what they are doing.

It was common for the person being crucified to speak from the cross, often with utterances of profanity or cursing, and pleas for clemency. During the six hours that Jesus remained alive on the cross, He uttered seven different "words" or statements. His final words were remarkable. The first three remarks, uttered as Jesus began His dreadful suffering, were directed towards the needs of others. A few utterances were no more than one word long. Only at the end, just before death, did Jesus address His own needs. Until that moment, He never failed to put others ahead of Himself with great love and compassion, even as He hung on the cross.

Jesus' first statement, recorded only by Luke, was directed towards the people who had persecuted Him. Jesus said, "Father forgive them for they do not know what they are doing" (Luke 23:34). Jesus uttered this prayer while He lay on the cross and the spikes were being driven into His hands and feet by the hammer. He repeated this prayer several times, expressing the urgency of His petition. The gospel makes it clear that Jesus greatly desired that those guilty individuals not be punished for their actions.

Jesus' prayer was very basic in form, though its contents were profound. It is important to note the three parts to this brief prayer. First, there was the word of invocation, or call to God, "Father." The invocation Jesus used was the intimate, familiar term that He taught His disciples to use in prayer to God. The relationship between Jesus and the Father was still intact during this part of the crucifixion, and so He called out to the loving Father for help for His executioners. The separation from the Father came later, during the hours of darkness from noon to three o'clock in the afternoon.

Next, there was the petition, "forgive them." Finally, there was the reason for His request, "they do not know what they are doing." It's astonishing that Jesus would make such a request for those who were acting so hatefully against Him. This reminds us of His word to the disciples in Matthew 5:44, as He says, ""But I tell you, love your enemies and pray for those who persecute you." Jesus was practicing what He preached. Jesus asked that the executioners en masse be absolved of their sins. Jesus wasn't forgiving the offenders by this prayer, but He was asking that something would be accomplished in the future so as to guarantee that they'd be forgiven. In other words, He was asking, "Father, please use my sacrifice in such a way so that these people might receive forgiveness."

It becomes clear that Jesus' prayer for forgiveness for those who persecuted Him was answered. The people who witnessed Jesus' death showed remorse as they dispersed from the crucifixion. Luke 23:48 says, "When all the people who had gathered to witness this sight saw what took place, they beat their breasts and went away." This expression of remorse or sorrow is the beginning of repentance (2 Corinthians 7:10). Even more significant, a large number of the priests present at Jesus' death came to believe in Him in the days afterward (Acts 6:7). Jesus' selfless prayer was answered at His crucifixion, and God continued to answer it after His Son was raised from the dead.

Personal Reflections

1. A similar prayer to Jesus' first statement on the cross was uttered by the first martyr in the infant church, Stephen. Stephen had preached a magnificent sermon in which he rehearsed the history of God's people throughout time. He then roundly condemned those who'd crucified Jesus, the people before whom he stood. The people were greatly offended by his accusations and rushed forward, dragging him out of the city, where they began to stone him. In Acts 7:60, we hear Stephen say, "Lord do not hold this sin against them." As Christians, we have sufficient evidence for praying in this manner when we're treated wrongfully by others. What is your usual reaction to mistreatment from others? How can you cultivate Jesus' and Stephen's spirit towards people who treat you unjustly?

2. This act of uttering a prayer repeatedly, as Jesus did before hanging on

the cross, was often called a "centering prayer" by Christian mystics of later ages. A centering prayer is comprised of a single sentence, which is repeated several times in order to clear the petitioner's thoughts, focusing their spirit and drawing them from the world into God's presence. As you enter into a time of prayer, you might use the following verses of scripture as a centering prayer to focus your thoughts on God:

Psalm 86:1
Hear me, Lord, and answer me, for I am poor and needy.

Psalm 88:2
May my prayer come before you; turn your ear to my cry.

Psalm 102:1
Hear my prayer, Lord; let my cry for help come to you

3. Christ tells us that as Christians, we should address God as "Father," even when we fall into sin or when we're suffering. It's important to maintain our sense of God in trying circumstances. Satan's mission is to attack our faith, causing us to doubt our salvation during the darkest moments in our lives. We must remember and embrace the truth that God is still our Father, regardless of the situation. We may think that He has turned against us and is judging us harshly, but it is not so. William Cowper captured this beautifully in one of his hymns:

Ye fearful saints fresh courage take; the clouds ye so much dread
Are big with mercy and shall break in blessing on your head.
Judge not the Lord by feeble sense but trust Him for His grace;
Behind a frowning providence He hides a smiling face.

God is faithful to His people, despite any doubt we have or sin we may commit. Do challenges exist to reform us, or are they sent to strengthen us, or both? Do you have a wise and mature Christian friend to consult when you're confused or in distress?

4. Jesus gave His followers a simple way to organize their prayers. A statement of adoration should precede a petition. This reminds us of the exalted One we are coming to. The great prayers recorded in Nehemiah 9,

and Daniel 9, among others, demonstrate this order. The men praise God in their opening statements of prayer, speaking of God's goodness, mercy, and love; they tell of His majesty and power. Only then do they make their requests to God. Why do you think petitions to God should mainly come after we remember how powerful, faithful, and loving He is?

Chapter 12

THE WORDS OF ACCEPTANCE

Matthew 27:39-44
Those who passed by hurled insults at him, shaking their heads
and saying, "You who are going to destroy the temple and build it
in three days, save yourself! Come down from the cross, if you are
the Son of God!" In the same way the chief priests, the teachers of
the law and the elders mocked him. "He saved others," they said,
"but he can't save himself! He's the king of Israel! Let him come
down now from the cross, and we will believe in him. He trusts in
God. Let God rescue him now if he wants him, for he said, 'I am
the Son of God.' " In the same way the rebels who were crucified
with him also heaped insults on him.

Luke 23: 39
One of the criminals who hung there hurled insults at him:
"Aren't you the Messiah? Save yourself and us!

As Jesus suffered on the cross, He continued to be subjected to insults,
ridicule and abuse. Those watching Him die challenged Him to prove who
He was and save Himself. The two thieves who were executed alongside
Jesus heard the verbal abuse from the crowd gathered there and joined in
with them. Despite the ceaseless mocking, Jesus refused to act out against
His persecutors.

Luke 23:40-41
But the other criminal rebuked him. "Don't you fear God," he
said, "since you are under the same sentence? We are punished
justly, for we are getting what our deeds deserve. But this man has
done nothing wrong.

Eventually, one thief ceased mocking Jesus and considered, perhaps for the
first time, who Jesus truly was. What could have caused this change in the

thief? Perhaps as he was led to his death, the thief learned that Jesus had been exchanged for Barabbas. Everyone knew that Barabbas was guilty of insurrection and murder (Luke 23:19), but possibly the thief only learned through the "grapevine" that Jesus had claimed to be God. Whatever the case, the thief eventually came to believe that Jesus was indeed the Son of God.

This thief had been close enough to hear Jesus' prayer for forgiveness as they were each placed on the cross. He may have wondered who this was, who could be so merciful to His executioners. This desire for forgiveness for the executioners was strange and very peculiar behaviour for a common criminal. There was a quietness about Jesus that was so starkly different from his words and that of the other thief being crucified. There was an acceptance and graciousness in Jesus that was most unusual given the circumstances. How could Jesus not be afraid in the face of death? Why did He not plead for mercy as the thieves did? Why wasn't Jesus angry with His accusers? Why did He not answer back to those who accused Him? These questions may have troubled the thief, causing him to reconsider Jesus' identity.

The thief may have also observed the sign on Jesus' cross, the one which indicated that He was King of the Jews. In confirmation of this message, a prophecy in the Old Testament states, "Rejoice greatly, Daughter Zion! Shout, Daughter Jerusalem! See, your king comes to you, righteous and victorious, lowly and riding on a donkey, on a colt, the foal of a donkey" (Zechariah 9:9). Perhaps the thief had heard this prophecy and witnessed Jesus' regal entry into Jerusalem atop a donkey. Somehow the Spirit of God opened the thief's eyes so he recognized Jesus as a king, righteous and gentle. If the thief were a Jew, he may have remembered the scripture taught to him by the rabbis as a boy, specifically the prophecy in Isaiah stating that God's servant would be numbered with the transgressors (Isaiah 53:12).

The thief certainly heard Jesus' enemies declare, "He saved others; let Him save Himself if He is the Son of God, the Chosen One" (Luke 23:35). Ironically, the thief learned from those who hated Jesus that He "saved others". If those who exulted in watching Jesus suffer acknowledged He was a Savior, perhaps it was true. The thief's confidence in Jesus' abilities may have been encouraged by the crowd's hostility around the cross and by the crowd's confession.

The man may have heard the angry crowd or the followers calling out, "Jesus," a name meaning "God saves." As it is written in Matthew 1:21, "You are to give him the name "Jesus" because He will save His people from their sins." Although the name "Jesus" was commonly used at that time, the criminal had certainly heard that this Jesus claimed to be God (Matthew 27:43).

Whatever took place that day, this thief was profoundly changed. He stopped mocking Jesus and turned to rebuke his fellow criminal. In effect, the believing thief told the other to consider his plight compared to that of Jesus. The two of them were receiving justice for their misdeeds whereas Jesus was innocent.

Luke 23:42-43
Then he said, "Jesus, remember me when you come into your kingdom." Jesus answered him, "Truly I tell you, today you will be with me in paradise.

After rebuking the other man, the thief turned to Jesus and prayed a most beautiful and humble prayer of faith: "Jesus, remember me when you come into your kingdom." When he asked to be remembered by Jesus, he meant much more than calling him to mind at some moment in the future. When the scriptures refer to God's remembrance of His covenant—for example, Psalm 106:45—it means that God gives attention to the covenant, a promise, and acts upon it. When it is said that God remembers His people's iniquity—for example, Hosea 7:2—it means that God punishes them for their sins. Therefore, in using the words "remember me," the thief was asking Jesus to remember his newfound faith and make him a part of His kingdom.

Jesus' gracious response was marvelous assurance, captured in the Gospel of Luke 23:43. It reads, "I tell you the truth, today you will be with me in Paradise." The thief's prayer had been heard, and it would be answered on that very day. He would be with Jesus in His heavenly kingdom. Through Jesus' declaration of mercy, He accepted the thief's request and granted him a place in the world to come.

Personal Reflections:

1. In John 14, Jesus told His disciples on the night of the betrayal that He was leaving to go and prepare a place for them. He promised to return and gather them to Himself, so they could live with Him forever. Jesus prayed that night, asking God that His followers would be with Him in the kingdom. It is clear that Jesus loved the company of His followers and desired an eternity with them, no matter what sins they had committed or who they were; this is a tangible representation of acceptance. Jesus offered the same acceptance to the thief dying on the cross beside Him. Throughout the Gospel of Luke in particular, we're told stories of Jesus interacting with the lowest and the most common of people. He's a friend to those whom many considered the dregs of society. He welcomes people that others reject. Looking at your own life, do you tend to practice acceptance? Are you willing to accept people whom others reject? Have you ever written off someone because of something that he or she did?

2. In scripture, God is happy to call us His "dearly loved children" (Ephesians 5:1) and "beloved" (Deuteronomy 33:12) to convey intimacy with us and genuine acceptance. We need to understand these words, recognizing the strong relationship that we may have with Him as Christians. In 1 Peter 5:5, we're told that "God opposes the proud, but shows favor to the humble." Knowing this, what things in your life get in the way of your relationship with God? In John 14:21 we're told, "Whoever has my commands and keeps them is the one who loves me. The one who loves me will be loved by my Father, and I too will love them and show myself to them." What other things can you do to improve your relationship with God?

Chapter 13

THE WORDS OF AFFECTION

John 19:25-27
Near the cross of Jesus stood his mother, his mother's sister,
Mary the wife of Clopas, and Mary Magdalene. When Jesus
saw his mother there, and the disciple whom he loved standing
nearby, he said to her, "Woman, here is your son," and to the
disciple, "Here is your mother." From that time on, this disciple
took her into his home.

As the eldest son in the family, Jesus had the responsibility of caring for
His mother if something happened to His legal father Joseph. Although
we're told that Joseph was a righteous man and that he loved Mary dearly
(Matthew 1:19), it was Jesus who acted as her sponsor and guardian
throughout His public ministry. This leads us to assume that Joseph had
died prior to the crucifixion, and so Jesus as the eldest son was responsible
for Mary's care.

In Jewish society at that time, adult children were expected to care for their
parents when the need arose. When Jesus taught the fifth commandment
concerning the honor given to one's mother and father, He insisted that
the word "honor" indicated that the children were obligated to support
their parents financially when necessary (Matthew 15:1-9).

Seeing Jesus on the cross, Mary would have recalled the day in the temple
when she and Joseph dedicated Him according to the Law of Moses
(Leviticus 12). This had taken place forty days after Jesus' birth. The
prophet Simeon took the infant in his arms and spoke frightening words
to Mary. He said, "This child is destined to cause the falling and rising of
many in Israel, and to be a sign that will be spoken against, so that the
thoughts of many hearts will be revealed. And a sword will pierce your own
soul too" (Luke 2:34-35). More than three decades later, Mary now would
have known exactly what the prophet had meant by the prediction he'd
made in the temple. She also would have known that Jesus was innocent

and didn't deserve to die. Those realities compounded her sorrow and the sword pierced her soul.

Thus, we are given these words of affection in the Gospel of John: "Dear woman, here is your son," uttered by Jesus as He hung on the cross. Even with the importance of Jesus' sacrifice and His unbelievable suffering, He didn't forget His mother. He loved her and was faithful and loyal to the end. Jesus not only graciously provided salvation for Mary, but understood that she needed relief from the awful scene at the cross. In the Scriptures, Mary isn't mentioned with the other women who were present when Jesus died (Matthew 27:56). The assumption is that John mercifully arranged for her to leave and took her away from the scene of suffering immediately. Jesus committed Mary into the hands of His beloved disciple for the rest of her life. Mary acquiesced to Jesus' wishes and that very hour withdrew to the disciple's home in Jerusalem.

Personal Reflections:

1. Jesus graciously set aside the horrors of the cross to care for His mother. This is a powerful demonstration of His affection and love for her. Moreover, He is demonstrating His faithfulness in serving His loved ones.

Jesus' example shows that we must adhere to the same faithfulness for our friends and family using our own talents and possessions. We shouldn't keep these to ourselves but use our resources for the good of others. This is what love is about. In 1 Corinthians 13:4-8, we see some of these characteristics of love: Love is kind; it protects, trusts, hopes, perseveres, and does not fail. Consider the relationships in your own family. Are you practicing the same kind of love towards your family that Jesus showed Mary as He was dying on the cross? What might you change to achieve this kind of love?

2. Mary knew her son was an innocent man. As a parent, guardian, friend or relative, how do you react when someone you love suffers unjustly? How do you feel when you have no way of intervening in their situation?

Chapter 14

THE WORDS OF ABANDONMENT

Matthew 27: 45-46
From noon until three in the afternoon darkness came over all the land. About three in the afternoon Jesus cried out in a loud voice, "Eli, Eli, lema sabachthani?" which means, "My God, my God, why have you forsaken me?"

Jesus' words of abandonment, shared in the gospels of Matthew and Mark, were probably uttered at about three o'clock in the afternoon, just before Jesus dismissed His spirit and died. Darkness had hung over the land since noon. The eerie gloom concerned the jeering mob around the cross, causing an uneasy silence. The blackness was an astronomical miracle.

Aside: Scientifically speaking, this period of darkness was too long to be a solar eclipse, which is a momentary phenomenon; it doesn't last for three hours rather a maximum of just over seven minutes. It was also the wrong time of the month for a solar eclipse. During Passover, there is a full moon positioned on the opposite side of the earth from the sun. For a solar eclipse to occur, the moon must pass between the sun and the earth.

At the time, Jews viewed darkness as a dreadful and abhorrent thing. If a Jew wanted to curse someone, he would speak of his lamp going out in darkness (Proverbs 20:20). When Zechariah spoke of those who were under the judgment of God, he referred to them as "those living in darkness and in the shadow of death" (Luke 1:79). From what we know about Jewish culture in Jesus' time, Jewish people would always light a lamp in their homes when the sun set and only extinguish it at sunrise of the next morning.

Jesus' cry of abandonment expressed the reality of His separation from God's presence, as well as being subjected to God's wrath during the time of darkness. Scripture states that being in God's presence and pleasing

God are closely linked. We see this in John 8:29, which reads, "The one who sent me is with me; He has not left me alone, for I always do what pleases Him." The one who pleases God will experience His presence.

In various places in Scripture, such as Job and the Psalms, we read of God's people in times of trial who feel as though they are deserted by God. They express their lament of abandonment openly in their suffering. As we read Psalm 22, for example, we hear the writer crying out in anguish that God has deserted him. At times, Scripture speaks as though God actually departs from His people: Ezekiel 9:9 notes, "The sin of the people of Israel and Judah is exceedingly great; the land is full of bloodshed and the city is full of injustice. They say, 'The Lord has forsaken the land; the Lord does not see.'" We see the same in Isaiah 59:2, which reads, "Your iniquities have separated you from your God." However, the promises of God remind us that He will never truly leave us (Matthew 28:20), despite the feeling of separation we may experience for a variety of reasons.

During Jesus' cry, He quotes from Psalm 22, not to describe a simple feeling of abandonment, but as an actual expression of reality. Bearing the accrued sins of His people, Jesus was separated from God's presence and subjected to His righteous wrath. The Old Testament, particularly the Book of Leviticus, clearly speaks about the substitution of one dying for others. In the Law of Moses, we read that the priest stands by a sacrificial animal and confesses the sins of the people (Leviticus 16:20). It is understood that the sins confessed are then transferred to the animal of sacrifice. Then, the animal is driven into the wilderness in permanent separation as it pictures the removal of the sins of the people. When completely abandoned by God, Jesus became the one true sacrifice for our sins, as expressed in 1 John 2:2: "He is the atoning sacrifice for our sins, and not only for ours, but also for the sins of the whole world." The same idea is expressed in Matthew 20:28, which reads, "The Son of Man did not come to be served but to serve, and to give His life as a ransom for many."

In 2 Corinthians 5:21, we are told that "God made Him who had no sin to be sin for us." 1 Peter 2:22 states that Jesus never committed sin; thus, when we learn about Jesus becoming sin, we understand that God laid our sins onto Him, akin to the symbolic transfer of sins onto the sacrificial lamb in Leviticus 16:20. Jesus was sacrificed on the cross in darkness while the goat was sent into the desert (Hebrews 10:1-4). It says in Deuteronomy 21:23, "anyone who is hung on a pole is under God's curse." This idea is explicitly quoted in reference to Jesus in Galatians 3:13: Jesus was under the curse of God while He bore our sins on the wooden cross. In John 10:11, Jesus proclaims, "I am the Good Shepherd. The Good Shepherd lays down His life for the sheep." The word "for" in this verse is very significant in the original Greek language of the Gospel of John. In Greek, the preposition "for" is "*huper*." Two accurate translations being "instead of" and "in the place of." Therefore, it is clear that Jesus died in the place of His sheep. Without Jesus' death, everyone would be condemned for their sins. As John the Baptist declared, "Look, the Lamb of God, who takes away the sin of the world!" (John 1:29).

In the Old Testament, God made covenants with various people. A covenant is a promise or an agreement between two or more people, yet God made a promise that He would take care of His people's needs in return for their faithfulness. In 2 Samuel 23:5, David says, "Has He not made with me an everlasting covenant, arranged and secured in every part?" The Scripture tells us, yes, God will not falter in His promise to us. However, Jeremiah 31:31-33 shares a new promise: "'The time is coming,' declares the Lord, 'when I will make a new covenant with the House of Israel and the House of Judah.... I will put my law in their minds and write it in their hearts. I will be their God and they will be my people."

This new covenant was an agreement between the Father and the Son before the world began that the Son would come to lead His people and die for them, as described in Ephesians 1:3-14. Furthermore, it says in Hebrews 9:15 that "Christ is the mediator of a new covenant." Namely, Jesus was promised to save humankind before the world was even created. According to 1 John 2:1, Jesus stands before God as the Advocate for His people. In the new covenant, we are promised that God will supply our needs through Jesus (Philippians 4: 19), so Jesus aids His people through daily tribulations as they make their way through this life in pursuit of the heavenly kingdom. In addition, the Holy Spirit came into the world to strengthen and prepare believers to overcome the various trials and temptations they face on their faith journey.

Earlier in His ministry, Jesus referred to His impending suffering on the cross when he said, "I have a baptism to undergo, and how distressed I am until it is completed!" (Luke 12:50). Jesus reaffirmed this notion in the Garden of Gethsemane as He said to Peter, James, and John, "My soul is overwhelmed with sorrow to the point of death.... Stay here and keep watch" (Mark 14:34). Shortly after, Luke tells us that, "being in anguish, Jesus prayed more earnestly, and His sweat was like drops of blood falling to the ground." (22:44) Jesus was so utterly distressed contemplating the coming punishment and rejection by God that He asked if He might let it pass.

Jesus cried out from the cross, "My God, my God, why have you forsaken me?" passionately demonstrating what He had previously verbalized in the Garden of Gethsemane. Only one who had known the fullness of God's love and favour could have experienced the inexplicable anguish of losing His presence. There is no greater humiliation or emotional strife than being rejected by the one you have dearly loved, faithfully served, and put first in your life. Jesus was completely and utterly abandoned by the one whom He loved greatly, His Father.

Personal Reflections:

1. There is a depth of meaning underpinning God's abandonment of Jesus that we Christians will never understand. Listening to Jesus' cry, we become eavesdroppers to a private communication between Him and His Father. Nevertheless, these words are recorded for all of us to consider. Jesus' sacrifice was for our sake and in our place. He didn't become a sinner on the cross, as in a person who committed acts of sin, He became sin. How can we strive to avoid sinfulness? How should we feel about our sins knowing how much they caused Jesus to suffer on the cross?

2. Sometimes in life we feel that God has forsaken us. Because Jesus has experienced true abandonment Himself, He is one to whom we can turn to express the pain and sorrow we feel. He invites us to approach Him with gracious words, such as, "Come to me, all you who are weary and burdened, and I will give you rest... for I am gentle and humble in heart, and you will find rest for your souls" (Matthew 11:28, 29). Why then are we sometimes reluctant to come before Jesus in a time of grief and aloneness? Do you doubt Jesus' understanding of what troubles you? Why? How can

we help one another overcome feelings of abandonment and encourage one another to reach out to Christ?

3. Only one thing is more detrimental than feeling the terror of being abandoned by God: Feeling abandoned by God and consciously withdrawing from Him and the hope He affords us. As we try to grasp the magnitude of Jesus' suffering, we need to remember the words of Isaiah 53:11: "After the suffering of His soul He will see the light of life and be satisfied." This passage in Isaiah explains that Jesus does not regret the punishment that He endured for us. He is satisfied to have gone through Hell and then ascended on our behalf. Moreover, He believes that we are worth what He experienced during those hours of pain and darkness. Truly, this is the extent of His love for us. Why, then, do we feel ill-treated when we have to endure emotional struggles? Why do we hesitate to suffer on Jesus' behalf? What does Hebrews 12:3 tell us about this dilemma when it says, "Consider Him who endured such opposition of sinners from sinful men, so that you will not grow weary and lose heart?"

Chapter 15

THE WORDS OF SUFFERING

John 19:28-29
Later, knowing that everything had now been finished, and so that Scripture would be fulfilled, Jesus said, "I am thirsty." A jar of wine vinegar was there, so they soaked a sponge in it, put the sponge on a stalk of the hyssop plant, and lifted it to Jesus' lips.

After Jesus had expressed the anguish of His spiritual suffering, He recognized the state of His physical agony. As seen in the Gospel of John, we witness the humanity of the Lord as He mentions His thirst. Jesus was fully human in addition to being fully God—one person with two natures. While here on earth, Jesus offered tangible, spiritual proof of His deity: He forgave sins (Mark 2:5), commanded the weather (Mark 4:39), raised the dead (John 11:43-44), read people's minds (Mark 2:8), and controlled demons (Mark 9:17-27), among other miracles. Jesus also provided concrete evidence of His humanity: He entered this world as a baby (Luke 2:7), demonstrated a human need to sleep (Mark 4:38), became hungry (Matthew 4:2), asked questions and learned (Luke 2:46), was tempted (Matthew 4:3), and, on the cross, became thirsty. The soldiers took pity on Jesus in His misery and shared their drink with Him—wine vinegar, a cheap drink popular among the poorer classes.

In Proverbs 17:22, it says, "A cheerful heart is good medicine, but a crushed spirit dries up the bones." Namely, intense suffering of the soul causes sickness in the body, and so Jesus' thirst was more than an ordinary thirst. Psalm 32:4 reiterates this notion by saying, "For day and night your hand was heavy upon me: my strength was sapped as in the heat of summer." Great spiritual suffering had compounded Jesus' physical thirst as He emerged from three, spiritless hours of the wrath and absence of God. There is an echo here in the words in Psalm 42:1-3, which reads, "As the deer pants for streams of water, so my soul pants for you, my God. My soul thirsts for God, for the living God. When can I go and meet with God? My tears have been my food day and night, while people say to me all day long, "Where is your God?"'

It is evident in the Gospel of John that Jesus gave careful attention to the Scriptures that prophesied the details of His suffering. Thus, it is concluded that Jesus spoke of His physical suffering on the cross so as to implement a prophecy concerning His punishment. Jesus could plainly see that He was "numbered with the transgressors," as Isaiah foretold (53:12), and as He listened to the scornful crowd before Him, He would have envisioned Psalm 22:7, which prophesied, "All who see me mock me; they hurl insults, shaking their heads." Mark 15:29, 30 elaborates on this verse, stating, "Those who passed by hurled insults at him, shaking their heads and saying, "So! You who are going to destroy the temple and build it in three days, come down from the cross and save yourself!"' Beyond the crowd, Jesus had witnessed the soldiers dividing His belongings between them, foretold in Scripture, as written in Psalm 22:18: "They divided my clothes among them and cast lots for my garment."

At that point, only one prophecy hadn't yet been fulfilled that spoke of His suffering prior to death. This detail is recorded in Psalm 69:21. "They put gall in my food and gave me vinegar for my thirst." In order to have this prophecy fulfilled, Jesus told the guards, "I thirst." Perhaps He had even seen the bottle of vinegar lying on the ground beneath Him. As John records in 19:29, "A jar of wine vinegar was there, so they soaked a sponge in it, put the sponge on a stalk of the hyssop plant, and lifted it to Jesus' lips." While Jesus refused to drink wine prior to the crucifixion, here, we witness that He drinks the liquid offered in order to ensure a total resolution of the prophecy. As He later explained to those whom He encountered after the resurrection, "This is what I told you while I was still with you: Everything must be fulfilled that is written about me in the Law of Moses, the Prophets and the Psalms" (Luke 24:44). Despite His immense physical and spiritual suffering borne on our behalf, Jesus' mind remained clear and dedicated to the scriptures until His death. He exercised total control of His faculties. He was triumphant!

Personal Reflections:

1. Jesus' knowledge of Scripture was a marvel of accuracy and detail. Faced

with unimaginable distractions, He neglected nothing that, regardless of how insignificant it seemed, was meant to be fulfilled according to the prophecies. With this realization, we should have great confidence in God's plan for us. Because God has honored His plan and stood by His immense promises in the past, we should place our trust in God's word regarding the future. More importantly, we ought to revere God's pledges to His people and affirm ourselves that His word is always righteous and true. There is great joy and comfort to be found in trusting God's plan and believing that He is faithful to our needs. God's name and reputation are both at stake in our lives, and His greatness is magnified as people witness the loyalty He shows to each of His pledges. Are you confident that God has a plan for everyone? Do you know God's plan for you? Are you confident that God will fulfill His promises to you? How does this chapter strengthen your trust in God?

2. As God's promises to His people are all certain, so are the warnings to those who do not trust in Him. God says that only in Jesus can we find our way back to Him. Those who trust in some other way will be disappointed in the end. God has spoken in scripture that Jesus is the perfect and only Savior. Only those, and all those, who come to God through Jesus will be received (John 14:6). Confirming this promise, Romans 10:13 notes, "Everyone who calls on the name of the Lord will be saved." Do you find yourself doubting that Jesus is the only way to God and Heaven? If so, why do you find this objectionable? How do you attempt to reach God?

Chapter 16

THE WORDS OF VICTORY

John 19:30
When He had received the drink, Jesus said, "It is finished!"

As we hear Jesus' words, "It is finished," reported to us by John, we must recognize that it has more than one meaning. On one hand, the utterance may be interpreted as a statement of resignation, or a sign of defeat. It is possible that Jesus was admitting the futility of His position, given the cruel treatment His enemies administered. The external circumstances all seemed to point to an inevitable end. His enemies were putting Him to death. His small band of followers had scattered and abandoned Him, faltering in the crisis of Gethsemane and ultimately leaving Him alone at the cross. There seemed to be nothing left of Jesus' mission or the movement He'd inspired. In this regard, Jesus may have been saying, "What's the use?"

Even with the theoretical possibility of this interpretation, based on the evidence at hand, we don't regard this interpretation as valid. On the contrary, Jesus was not losing hope in His mission or renouncing His followers. No, the words, "it is finished," are a triumphant and exhilarated expression of victory over sin. The question now is, "What is finished?"

One very popular and long-accepted interpretation is that Jesus was rejoicing that the great work of redemption was complete; He had finished all that His Father had sent Him to do. However, we need to recognize that at this specific moment, He hadn't yet accomplished all that had been prophesied about Him nor all that He had prophesied about Himself. He had yet to die (Isaiah 53:12). His body had yet to be pierced with a spear (Zechariah 12:10) with no bones broken (Psalm 34:20). He had yet to be buried with the rich (Isaiah 53:9). He had yet to remain in the grave for three days' time (Matthew 17:23). He had yet to rise again (Matthew 28:6), and He had yet to ascend to God, the Father (John 14:2). With these things considered, we have considerable reason to believe that Jesus was determined to satisfy the remaining prophecies from Scripture.

While the prophecies were not yet all fulfilled, Jesus' life and sacrifice had completed a great part of His mission. Throughout the days of the Old Testament, the Jews made sacrifices for sin that did not actually absolve their misdeeds. Jesus was the Lamb of God that would be sacrificed to take away the sins of God's people for eternity. As it is written in Hebrews 10:14, "By one sacrifice He has made perfect forever those who are being made holy." The word "finished" does not simply mean "over"; it is also understood to mean "paid in full." Jesus was destined to die and rise again, but with His sacrifice for us completed, our debt was paid in full. Jesus was victorious!

Personal Reflections:

1. One thing is certain: What God starts, He finishes. God never attempts anything. He accomplishes all that He promises to do. Therefore, we can be very confident that He will bring to completion all that concerns those who trust in Him. If you have become a Christian, you may be sure that the Lord is going to continue to work in your life until His specific plan for you is complete (Philippians 1:6). "For it is God who works in you to will and to act in order to fulfill his good purpose" (Philippians 2:13). You are not an attempt by God; you are an accomplishment of God. Do you believe that God guides you in your own, specific walk? Do you doubt that there is a mission for you? Do you know your mission? Do you treat yourself as an attempt or an accomplishment? Why?

2. With the completion of Jesus' sacrifice, we are free from sin! We need not fear the sins of our past; our souls have been wiped clean. We are released from those sins and any penalties in consequence. Unfortunately, people often revisit their past wrongs, dig them up, inspect them, and ruminate on them. If God has forgotten our sins and put them behind Him, why cannot we? Why do we continue to punish ourselves (and others) for the sins we have committed? What should we do in order to forgive ourselves for sinning? What can we do to stop ourselves from punishing ourselves like this?

Chapter 17

THE WORDS OF COMMITMENT

Luke 23:46
Jesus called out with a loud voice, "Father into your hands I
commit my spirit." When He had said this, He breathed His last.

In His final words, provided to us by Luke, Jesus summoned a divine
strength and shouted triumphantly that He was returning to God's light.
There is a spirit of confidence in this moment as Jesus knows that God is
willing to receive Him once more. There is immediacy to this reception,
for the person leaves his earthly house (the body) and enters directly into
God's presence. In 2 Corinthians 5:6-8 it says, "Therefore, we are always
confident and know that as long as we are at home in the body, we are away
from the Lord.... We are confident, I say, and would prefer to be away from
the body and at home with the Lord." It was confidence in this message
that gave Jesus the strength to speak His final words so joyfully.

In Jesus' final statements, He made certain that Scripture was His final
word on the cross. Here, He quoted Psalm 31:5, a bedtime prayer that
mothers of Jesus' day would teach to their children when they were first
learning to speak. Mary likely taught this prayer in Psalm 31:5 to Jesus as
a child in the Jewish tradition. The term "Father" is not in the Psalm, but
Jesus taught us to address God as Father in order to enhance our spiritual
relationship.

Aside: The Psalms hold great comfort for God's people because they speak
very intimately of God and His love for His children. For those who are
tired and weary in the battle, the Psalms have special relevance, as the
writers poured out their own complaints to God and found comfort in
drawing near to Him and recalling His faithfulness. No wonder Jesus
quoted these verses at such a moment.

Jesus' addressed His final words to the "Father," the most intimate name for

God. His previous stark outcry, "My God, My God," gave way to this warm expression of security and love. Once again, Jesus was in a relationship and fellowship with God. The curse He was under during the hours of darkness had been lifted. Galatians 3:13 tells us that He had been made a curse for us, but now it had lifted, and He was free from it. Soon, Jesus would be in Paradise awaiting the repentant thief's arrival, as promised.

Then, as we read in Luke 23:46, Jesus breathed His last, literally meaning that He dismissed His spirit. By an act of will, Jesus caused the separation of His body and spirit. This is something that no person can do solely through an act of will. People can summon death only by physical means. Jesus had said that no one would take His life from Him but that He would lay down His life Himself (John 10:17-18). True to His word, Jesus laid down His life for His sheep.

Personal Reflections:

1. The confidence that Jesus displayed in His final words is the same confidence instilled into every Christian's heart. The Holy Spirit enters the Christian's life and assures the individual that he or she is a child of God. God's peace and love are poured out into the person's heart by this same Spirit. It is the Spirit that encourages Christians to believe, "Precious in the sight of the Lord is the death of His faithful servants" (Psalm 116:15). Do you fear death? Are you worried that you won't be prepared for it when it comes? How can you embrace the Holy Spirit to prepare for this time?

2. Pastors throughout the centuries have taught church members to repeat Jesus' last words from the cross while in their final hours of life: "Father, into your hands I commit my spirit." Dying Christians can speak these words with confidence to the One who sent His Son to die for them and rise again, the One whom they will see upon departing the body. In fact, many famous Christians throughout history took spiritual refuge in these same words and found strength in the final moments of their own earthly pilgrimages; including: John Hus, Martin Luther, Philip Melanchthon, and others. It's marvelous to consider that when death comes, we meet our Father in Heaven, just as Jesus did.

Here is the heart's true home, the place of refuge and safety in the presence of God. Death's only power is to offer Christians a greater sense of God's presence than was ever experienced in this life. Just as the horror of Hell is not the flames but the absence of God, so the glory of Heaven is not the streets of gold but the glorious and immediate presence of the Lord Himself. In eternal life, we shall find ourselves filled with the knowledge of God. As it says in John 17:3, "Now this is eternal life: that they may know you, the only true God, and Jesus Christ, whom you have sent." Additionally, Revelation 14:13 reads, "Blessed are the dead who die in the Lord." What do you think is so precious about ascending into eternal life? Do you feel that the value of eternal life is built upon quality or quantity?

3. We must keep the truth of God as our Father perpetually in our hearts and minds. When we come to realize it, we will want to use our lives on earth to honor and reflect our appreciation for His grace. We express our dedication by how we pray, beginning with "Our Father" (Matthew 6:9). This simple phrase is the way in which to view the world and all that is in it. The world belongs to our Father in Heaven (Psalm 24:1). It is how we should see eternity, as in "my Father's house has many rooms." (John 14:2). We Christians dare to draw near to Jesus and address God as our own Father. There is an expression that goes, "He is so heavenly-minded that he is no earthly good." On the other hand, some people are so earthly-minded that they are no heavenly good. What does this notion mean to you? When Colossians 3:2 says, "Set your mind on things above, not on earthly things," how does this verse apply to you? Do you have your heart set too much on earthly things? How can you change this?

Chapter 18

IN CONCLUSION

As we draw to the end of our journey with the Savior many thoughts come to mind. We have considered some of the historical background to these sacred events and probed our innermost thoughts and convictions in the Reflections.

Meditating on the last hours of our Lord's life and how truly magnificent and triumphant He was surely we should cry out with the words of the centurion who superintended our Lord's final hours. Mark 15:39 "And when the centurion, who stood there in front of Jesus, saw how he died, he said, 'Surely this man was the Son of God!'"

The One Who called Himself "the Truth" (John 14:6) was branded as a liar and imposter by His enemies. Yet when He was tried for deception and blasphemy He was triumphant. His majestic manner and calm spirit attained through His prayers in Gethsemane contradicted the deceit and vicious cruelty of His enemies.

As we peruse the pages of this book we find many points to ponder, and details to draw us out in worship of the One Who loved us and gave Himself for us. I invite my readers to review the quoted Scriptures and commentary and allow the message to fill your hearts with joyful adoration of the King of kings and Lord of lords.

As you rethink the Reflections may you be encouraged to renew your efforts to follow your Savior's example. Through imitation of His gracious actions may you exalt Him by the life you live.

Charles Wesley put it well in one of his hymns as he described the present experience of believers and their final destiny when he wrote:

> Changed from glory into glory,
> Till in Heav'n we take our place,
> Till we cast our crowns before Thee,
> Lost in wonder, love, and praise.

My sole purpose in writing this book has been to so present the Lord Jesus Christ that the reader would experience the exhortation found in 2 Peter 3:18.

"Grow in the grace and knowledge of our Lord and Savior Jesus Christ. To him be glory both now and forever! Amen."

CPSIA information can be obtained at www.ICGtesting.com
Printed in the USA
LVOW06s2347221015

459382LV00001B/35/P